NOBEL PRIZE-WINNING

SCIENTISTS

GUGLIELMO MARCONI

INVENTOR OF RADIO AND WIRELESS COMMUNICATION

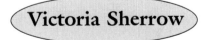

Victoria Sherrow

Enslow Publishers, Inc.

40 Industrial Road   PO Box 38
Box 398   Aldershot
Berkeley Heights, NJ 07922   Hants GU12 6BP
USA   UK

http://www.enslow.com

"There can be no doubt that wireless telegraphy . . . has come to stay, and will not only stay but continue to advance."

—**Guglielmo Marconi**

Library of Congress Cataloging-in-Publication Data

Sherrow, Victoria.
  Guglielmo Marconi : inventor of radio and wireless communication / Victoria Sherrow.
      p. cm. — (Nobel Prize-winning scientists)
    Includes bibliographical references and index.
    ISBN 0-7660-2280-3
    1. Marconi, Guglielmo, marchese, 1874-1937—Juvenile literature.
  2. Inventors—Italy—Biography—Juvenile literature. 3. Telegraph, Wireless—Italy—History—Juvenile literature. 4. Radio—Italy—History—Juvenile literature.
  I. Title. II. Series.
  TK5739.M3S54 2004
  621.384'092—dc22

                                    2004001735

Printed in the United States of America

10 9 8 7 6 5 4 3 2 1

To Our Readers:
We have done our best to make sure all Internet Addresses in this book were active and appropriate when we went to press. However, the author and the publisher have no control over and assume no liability for the material available on those Internet sites or on other Web sites they may link to. Any comments or suggestions can be sent by e-mail to comments@enslow.com or to the address on the back cover.

Illustration Credits: ArtToday.com, pp. 39, 59, 67, 83; Enslow Publishers, Inc., p. 96; Library of Congress, pp. 11, 75, 90.

Cover Illustration: Library of Congress (inset); Enslow Publishers, Inc. (background).

CONTENTS

THE NOBEL PRIZE

Every year since its founding in 1901, the Nobel Prize has been awarded to individuals who have distinguished themselves in the fields of physiology or medicine, physics, chemistry, literature, and peace. (In 1968 a prize for economics was added.) The prize is named for Alfred Nobel, a Swede born in Stockholm in 1833, who grew up to become a successful chemist, manufacturer, and businessman.

Nobel began experimenting with ways to make nitroglycerine safer for practical use. Eventually he found a way to mix nitroglycerine with silica and make a paste. He could then shape the paste into a stick that could be placed in holes drilled in rocks. He patented this creation in 1867 and named it dynamite. In order to detonate the dynamite sticks, Nobel also invented a blasting cap that could be ignited by burning a fuse. The invention of dynamite, along with equipment like the diamond drilling crown and the pneumatic drill, significantly reduced the expenses associated with many types of construction work.

Soon Nobel's dynamite and blasting caps were in great demand. Nobel proved to be an astute businessman, establishing companies and laboratories throughout the world. He also continued to experiment with other chemical inventions and held more than 350 patents in his lifetime.

Alfred Nobel did not narrow his learning just to scientific knowledge. His love of literature and poetry prompted him to write his own works, and his social conscience kept him interested in peace-related issues.

When Nobel died on December 10, 1896, and his will was read, everyone was surprised to learn that he left instructions that the accumulated fortune from his companies and business ventures (estimated at more than $3 million U.S.) was to be used to award prizes in physics, chemistry, physiology or medicine, literature, and peace.

In fulfilling Alfred Nobel's will, the Nobel Foundation was established in order to oversee the funds left by Nobel and to coordinate the work of the prize-awarding institutions. Nobel prizes are presented every December 10, the anniversary of Alfred Nobel's death.

A COMMUNICATIONS GIANT

The thirty-five-year-old man standing at the podium in Stockholm, Sweden, on the evening of December 11, 1909, was slight of build, with a modest demeanor. He had no university degree and was largely self-taught. Yet people around the world knew his name—Guglielmo Marconi— for he was a giant in the field of communications. While still in his twenties, Marconi had devised a practical method of sending messages at the speed of light, across thousands of miles, without any wires or other physical connection between sender and receiver. Now he had come to Sweden to accept the prestigious Nobel Prize for Physics in recognition of his work.

At the award ceremony, Dr. H. Hildebrand, President of the Royal Swedish Academy of Sciences, praised Marconi's achievement, saying, "Research workers and engineers toil unceasingly on the development of wireless telegraphy.

Where this development can lead, we know not. However, with the results already achieved, telegraphy over wires has been extended by this invention in the most fortunate way. Independent of fixed conductor routes and independent of space, we can produce connections between far-distant places, over far-reaching waters and deserts."[1]

Today, people tend to take long-distance wireless communication for granted. We are accustomed to radio, television, mobile telephones, and fax machines, as well as radar, radio-navigation systems, satellite communications, and telescopes that visit outer space and send information about other planets back to Earth. We can hear about the news as soon as it happens—and even see it happening, right before our eyes on the television screen. We can call people throughout the world, for business or personal reasons, and send "instant messages" via the Internet.

None of these modern conveniences existed at the dawn of the twentieth century. Although people of that era could communicate by telegraph and telephone, both methods required wires and had a limited range. During the late 1800s, most of the world's top scientists and engineers scoffed at the idea that messages could travel long distances without wires, especially over the earth's horizon. They believed signals would simply "disappear" into the air. According to these experts, wireless communication was impossible.

Guglielmo Marconi had been just as firmly convinced that it *was* possible, and he set out to prove it. In 1894, after reading about Heinrich Hertz's work with long wavelength electromagnetic radiation, Marconi began experimenting with these invisible waves, which became known as "radio waves."

Over the next six years, Marconi built equipment that could transmit electrical signals without wires. He managed to send these signals from one end of a table to the other . . . then across a field . . . and even across the English Channel. In December 1901, he awed people around the world by sending wireless messages across the Atlantic Ocean. Like Thomas Edison, Samuel Morse, Henry Ford, Alexander Graham Bell, and the Wright Brothers, the name of Guglielmo Marconi was now associated with an amazing new invention.

The years just before and after 1900 brought many historic and life-changing developments, including air flight, automobiles, mass production, and wireless communication. Since the beginning of time, humans have looked for new and better ways to communicate. The earliest humans used simple methods, such as sign language and pictures, to share information, ideas, and feelings. Verbal communication was only possible when people shared a common language and were close enough to exchange words. As they formed larger communities and nations, people wanted to make contact across long distances. They could write messages, which must then be delivered, or use fire and smoke signals that could be seen in the distance. Ships carried flags with different colors and designs and, later, lighted lamps to signal other ships or people at the port, while lighthouses warned vessels. As rail transportation developed, signaling systems were also devised for trains.

Methods for sending and receiving messages remained relatively unchanged until the nineteenth century, when people began learning more about the energy force called electricity. By the time Marconi was a young man living in Italy in the 1880s, the building blocks for wireless telegraphy had been steadily developing. People from different countries contributed scientific theories and equipment. Like pieces of a puzzle, they waited and hoped for people with patience and vision to put them together in a practical way.

Marconi later said that it was "impossible" to know in those early days what he would eventually accomplish, "but even when I had only succeeded in sending and receiving signals across a few yards of space by means of Hertzian waves I had the vision of communication by this means over unlimited distances. To have made such claims at that time would have been to invite the ridicule of scientists, as, indeed, was proved when, five years later, I had the faith to believe that by means of the system I had evolved it would be possible to send and receive signals across the Atlantic Ocean."[2]

Marconi's system of wireless telegraphy brought him international acclaim, wealth, and the prestigious Nobel Prize for physics, which he shared with German physicist Ferdinand Braun. Both men were recognized for significant achievements in the field of wireless telegraphy. In presenting the joint award, the Nobel citation noted the important practical applications of the wireless. Certainly, it had made sea travel safer. In 1901, the passenger ship *Campania* became the first ship to be equipped with a Marconi radio; by 1909 all of the major naval forces in the world and 300 merchant ships and liners had a wireless device on board. The capacity to access help quickly during a disaster, by

THE INVENTOR OF WIRELESS COMMUNICATION, GUGLIELMO MARCONI.

contacting land-based stations or other ships, was saving lives.

At the Nobel Prize ceremony, Marconi gave his lecture in English, which he spoke fluently. He noted that the field of wireless communication was still evolving, saying, "Whatever may be its present shortcomings and defects, there can be no doubt that wireless telegraphy—even over great distances—has come to stay, and will not only stay but continue to advance."[3] He went on to explain the process he had used over the years to develop his wireless, then described the potential for new theories, technology, and discoveries that could improve wireless communication in the future.

While Marconi was relatively well-known, few people outside Germany or the scientific community knew much about the fifty-nine-year-old Braun, who had developed a cathode ray indicator tube (CRT) in 1897. Braun's CRT included a fluorescent screen—called the cathode ray oscilloscope—that could emit a visible light when it was struck by a beam of electrons. Though people did not realize it at the time, this invention would later play a key role in the development of television. In 1898, Braun began working on wireless telegraphy and found ways to modify the transmitter so that aerial transmissions could be received over longer distances. The improvements Braun made in both transmitters and receivers produced stronger signals and increased both the range and the privacy of radio signals.

The Nobel committee declared that both Marconi and Braun had helped to develop vital new technology. Praising Marconi's work, the Nobel committee noted, "A man was needed who was able to grasp the potentialities of the enterprise and who could overcome all the various difficulties which stood in the way of the practical realization of the idea. The carrying out of this great task was reserved for Guglielmo Marconi . . . the first success was gained as a result of his ability to shape the whole thing into a practical, usable system, added to his inflexible energy with which he pursued his self-appointed aim."[4]

This joint Nobel prize aroused some controversy, however. Because Braun's work was less famous, some critics said that Marconi alone deserved the honor. A humorous cartoon that appeared in a Swedish newspaper showed Marconi saying, "I can't seem to place him," while Braun responded, "I am well known."[5] Yet the two men were friendly when they met. In her 1962 biography of her father, Marconi's daughter Degna wrote, "Braun charmingly apologized for being there at all and expressed the feeling that the whole award should go to Father."[6] For his part, Marconi praised Braun's work and the two honorees enjoyed discussing their mutual interests.

At the awards ceremony, Dr. H. Hildebrand, President of the Royal Swedish Academy of Sciences, explained the Nobel committee's decision to honor both men: "Marconi's original system had its weak points. The electrical oscillations sent out from the transmitting station were relatively weak and consisted of wave-series following each other, of which the amplitude rapidly fell—so-called 'damped oscillations.' A result of this was that the waves had a very weak effect at the receiving station, with the further result that waves from various other transmitting stations readily interfered."[7]

Hildebrand said that Braun's "inspired work" resolved that problem. He declared that "Braun made a modification in the layout of the circuit for the [dispatch] of electrical waves so that it was possible to produce intense waves with very little damping. It is only through the introduction of these improvements that the magnificent results in the use of wireless telegraphy have been attained in recent times."[8]

As a child, Marconi had been a rather mediocre student whose experiments antagonized his father. As a young man, his ideas defied the scientific thinking of his era. Yet Guglielmo Marconi was destined to develop and promote an amazing invention that would change communication forever.

CHAPTER TWO

BIG EARS AND BIG IDEAS

To develop his wireless, Marconi would need determination and an independent mind, plus the ability to blend theoretical knowledge with practical skills. His family background and upbringing fostered these traits, as well as a head for business and social connections that helped him to market his inventions.

His father, Giuseppe Marconi, was a wealthy estate owner and businessman from a small Appenine mountain community located between Florence and Bologna. As a young man, Giuseppe briefly studied for the priesthood until he decided that it was not his true calling. After supervising his family's small farm for a few years, he moved to Bologna in central Italy, where he met Giulia de Renoli, a banker's daughter. They were married in 1855, but she died less than a year later while giving birth to their son, Luigi. Alone with an infant, Giuseppe invited his widowed father, Domenico, to live with him, and they bought a country home called the Villa Griffone in Pontecchio, outside

Bologna. There, Domenico founded a successful silkworm business while Giuseppe developed the land. After Domenico died, Giuseppe remained with Luigi at the villa, where he managed the thriving vineyards and other crops grown on the estate.

Giuseppe's second wife, Annie Jameson, grew up in Ireland and was seventeen years his junior. This unlikely couple met in 1864 after a series of events brought Annie to Italy. She and her two sisters enjoyed a comfortable life in Dublin, where her Scottish father had founded a lucrative brewery business with his brothers. A talented singer, Annie hoped to perform on stage, but her parents considered a professional singing career unsuitable for a woman of her social class. To soothe their ambitious daughter, they agreed she could spend some time studying opera in Bologna, Italy, where she would live with their banking friends—who happened to be Giuseppe Marconi's in-laws, the de Renolis. After meeting at their home, Annie and Giuseppe fell in love.

Back in Ireland, Annie's parents forbade her to marry this "foreigner," who was already a father and in his thirties. She returned home and pretended to respect their wishes but inwardly resolved to follow her heart. Showing the determined spirit that her son would later display, Annie Jameson made secret plans to reunite with Giuseppe the next year when she turned eighteen and no longer needed her parents' permission to marry. In 1865, the couple met again, this time in France, where they were wed before returning to Bologna. Although the Jamesons had opposed the marriage, they accepted their daughter's decision and her new husband.

A year later, Annie gave birth to Alfonso, and nine years later, on April 25, 1874, the Marconis welcomed their second child, another son. Guglielmo, who had his mother's blue eyes and fair coloring, was born at the family's townhouse, the Palazzo Marescalchi in Piazza San Salvatora, near the Bologna city hall. A family legend says that when the Marconis' old gardener saw the new baby for the first time, he exclaimed, "What big ears he has!" and his proud mother made this visionary remark: "He will be able to hear the still, small voice of the air."[1] Other people also noticed baby Guglielmo's large ears, but nobody could have predicted that someday he would use them to detect a faint clicking noise that meant wireless signals had crossed the Atlantic Ocean.

A few weeks after Guglielmo's birth, the Marconis left their townhouse to spend the summer at the Villa Griffone. As he grew up, Guglielmo enjoyed the beautiful gardens, lush lemon and chestnut groves, fields of grazing animals, and mountain views surrounding the stately stone house. There were fields to explore and lakes where the Marconi boys could swim, boat, and fish.

Travel was also part of Guglielmo's life. At age three, he visited relatives in England for the first time, and, through the years, he became familiar with different regions in Italy. Annie Marconi disliked cold weather, so when winter arrived she left Bologna for a warmer climate—usually Florence or Leghorn (Livorno), on Italy's west coast, along the Mediterranean Sea. Although Giuseppe often stayed at home to work, Annie had the company of her sister, Elizabeth Prescott, who was living in Leghorn with her four daughters while her husband was stationed with

British troops in India. There was an English colony in Leghorn and a Waldesian Church, which Annie attended with her sons. Though Giuseppe was a Catholic and Alfonso and Guglielmo had been baptized in that church, they were reared in their mother's Protestant faith. In the evenings, Annie read to them in English from the King James Bible. Both boys grew up learning English and Italian.

It was at Leghorn that Guglielmo acquired his lifelong love for the sea. He learned to sail at age nine and received his own boat when he reached his early teens. Though somewhat of a loner, he enjoyed playing with his cousins, especially Daisy, and he loved music, an interest his mother encouraged. Above all, Guglielmo enjoyed learning. He was often on his own, because he was much younger than Alfonso and his half-brother Luigi, and no other children his age lived near the villa. Yet he was not bored or lonely because he was curious about many things and enjoyed studying them by reading, thinking, observing, and experimenting.

As a child, Guglielmo attended elementary schools in Casalecchio and Reno, but his mother also hired tutors because the family did not live in one place year-round. After he learned to read, Guglielmo spent hours each day with books. Greek myths and Greek history were his first loves, but he began favoring books about science and machinery, such as steam engines. Two of his heroes were Benjamin Franklin, the American statesman, scientist, and inventor, and English scientist Michael Faraday. He tackled increasingly difficult books about physical and electrical science as he discovered the work of scientists from different countries. In his Nobel lecture in 1909, Marconi would recall those days, saying, "I never studied physics or electrotechnics in the regular manner, although as a boy I was deeply interested in those subjects."[2]

By the 1880s, scientists had learned intriguing things about electricity as they proposed various theories and conducted experiments. They created tools to study electrical phenomena, such as the Leyden jar, which a Dutch professor named Peiter van Musschenbroek developed in 1745. He partially filled a cylindrical glass jar with water and placed a thick conducting wire inside. One end of the wire was pulled through a cork that sealed the jar's opening, then charged with a friction device that produced static electricity. Other scientists improved on Leyden jars, which provided the means to build and store electric energy.

In 1799–1800, the Italian scientist Alessandro Volta (1745–1827) made what is regarded as the first battery. He found that he could create electricity by combining certain metals (in this case, copper and zinc) with chemicals (an acid), thereby changing chemical energy into electrical energy. Volta's electricity-producing cell was called a voltaic pile or battery, and the word "volt," a unit of electrical energy, comes from his name.

In 1820, Hans Oersted (1777–1851) of Denmark discovered a close relationship between electricity and magnetism. Oersted found that electricity traveling through a wire could move the needles on a compass, which meant that the wire acted as a magnet, or electromagnet. The electrified wire was actually surrounded by a magnetic field. Andre-Marie Ampere (1775–1836) expanded on Oersted's work by demonstrating that two wires carrying electricity would interact magnetically. During a series of experiments, Ampere saw that parallel currents (those flowing in the same direction) attract each other, while anti-parallel currents (those flowing in opposite directions) repel each other.

Meanwhile, in 1825, British scientist William Sturgeon built a practical electromagnet. When electricity ran through his U-shaped magnet, it was able to lift objects ten times its own weight. Magnetism could be used to produce electricity and vice versa. Joseph Henry (1797–1878) further illuminated the links between these forces and determined that an electric current flowing through a wire creates a magnetic field around that wire. He found ways to avoid short-circuits by insulating the wires on his electromagnets. Furthermore, Henry's experiments showed that if the current flowing through the wire was constantly changing, it could produce an electric current in another wire nearby, even though the wires were not connected. Later, this knowledge would be used to develop motors, generators, transformers, telephones, and other devices.

In the meantime, Michael Faraday (1791–1867) turned his quick mind to electric phenomena. A blacksmith's son, Faraday had to quit school at age thirteen to become a bookbinder's apprentice, but the customers in the shop noticed his intelligence and encouraged him to study, and he was excused from work to attend science lectures. The famous chemist Humphry Davy made him an assistant at the Royal Institute in 1812, and Faraday went on to do his own original research. In 1832, he wrote: "I cannot but think that the action of electricity and magnetism is propagated through space in some form of vibration."[3] While investigating this possibility, Faraday invented a method of electromagnetic induction and found a way to produce a steady current.

Guglielmo also read about James Clerk Maxwell (1831–1879), a Scottish scientist who developed the first radiowave theorum. In 1864, Maxwell suggested that changes in the amount of electricity traveling along a wire will send "waves" into the air, much like waves rippling across the water. Furthermore, said Maxwell, light must be an electromagnetic vibration—a different version of the same phenomenon—and electrical "waves" must travel at the speed of light.

In 1873, Maxwell showed mathematically that electric waves are a form of electromagnetism. These mathematical equations laid the foundation for modern electronics, and the invisible waves became known as Maxwell's waves. A unit of measurement called the wavelength was used to measure them, showing the distance from a point on one wave (e.g., the peak) to that same point on the next wave.

In the decades that followed, scientists would discover that heat, X rays, and microwaves were also electromagnetic phenomena. During the early 1900s, they would measure the speed of light—186,291 miles per second (299,792 km per second)—which means that light can circle the earth seven and one half times in one second!

Guglielmo Marconi was excited by what he read and wanted to see for himself how things worked. He began taking apart mechanical devices and putting them back together. By age ten, he had built some scientific toys and gadgets of his own, including a roasting spit. His daughter Degna later wrote, "His chubby little-boy hands, later so strong and quick, were already nimble. He loved to use them on machinery and always had some project going."[4]

Annie Marconi encouraged Guglielmo, but his father considered his son's activities to be wasteful and pointless. Giuseppe was a strict father who expected his children to appear promptly for meals and other activities, be neat and clean, and follow his instructions. He also thought Guglielmo should read less and spend more time outdoors. When Annie defended him, Giuseppe pointed out that their youngest son's schoolwork did not improve, despite the many hours that he spent reading and making machines. In fact, it seemed to distract him from his academic studies.

Some experiments enraged his father. One of them occurred after Guglielmo read about Benjamin Franklin's work with static electricity. During one famous experiment, Franklin flew a kite during a thunderstorm. When the metal key he had attached to the kite was on the ground, electric sparks flew from it, proving that lightning was a form of electricity. In 1750, Franklin wrote a letter to the Royal Society of London, suggesting that "electrical fire" might "be drawn from a cloud silently, before it could come close enough to strike."[5]

Guglielmo tried some electricity experiments of his own. In another experiment, he lined up rows of dinner plates on the edge of a stream and shot high-voltage electricity through them, which made them crash into the water and shatter. His father complained bitterly about this waste of household goods, and even threw out some of Guglielmo's projects. As a result, Guglielmo became more secretive about his activities. He grew even closer to his mother, and more distant from his father, though his mother could not prevent all of their conflicts.

Because Giuseppe Marconi was almost fifty years old when Guglielmo was born and spent so much time running the estate, Annie Marconi played the chief role in raising her sons. She respected Guglielmo's ideas and nurtured his curiosity and imagination. Years later, Marconi's daughter Degna recalled Annie's philosophy about child rearing, which she expressed in comments like this: "If only grownups understood what harm they can do children. They think nothing of constantly interrupting their train of thought."[6] For his part, Guglielmo tried to avoid trouble and found ways to "obey" his father while pursuing his interests. When he was ordered outdoors, he often chose to go fishing so that he could continue thinking about his projects while he waited for fish to snatch the bait.

In 1886, twelve-year-old Guglielmo received his elementary school diploma. He was then enrolled at the Instituto Cavallero on the Via delle Terme in Florence. Shy by nature, Guglielmo could get along with people but preferred one-on-one friendships over groups, so he found it difficult to fit in, as he had in primary school. Other students teased him, possibly because he was more serious and solitary than his peers. Professors and schoolmates also criticized his Italian, which did not sound the same as theirs.

Guglielmo was willing to work hard, but only if the subject really interested him. When it did, he was able to concentrate and learn a subject thoroughly—qualities that would help him to succeed once he set a goal. Two courses at the institute truly interested him: physics and chemistry.

CHAPTER THREE

A DREAM TAKES SHAPE

After his frustrating year in Florence, Marconi was relieved when his family decided to rent a home in Leghorn the next year. This meant that he could attend a different school: the Instituto Nazionale (National Institute), which was a private technical school. Marconi enjoyed his classes and earned better grades than he had before, though he did not complete the full curriculum and therefore never received a diploma.

That year, his life expanded socially as well as academically. He made friends with the boy next door, Giulio Camperio, a fellow science lover who also attended the institute. Marconi's Italian improved as he spent time with Giulio and his sister. He also enjoyed visiting Nello Marchetti, an elderly man who had worked as a telegraph operator. Marchetti taught him Morse code, something he would later use in his work with the wireless.

Annie Marconi continued to oversee her sons' education. When she decided they should learn a musical instrument,

Guglielmo began piano lessons and continued to play the piano throughout his life. To nurture his scientific interests, his mother arranged for him to study privately with Professor Vincenzo Rosa, a respected physicist and instructor at the Liceo Niccolini in Leghorn. Marconi later recalled the "clear and practical method with which Professor Rosa started me in the study of electrophysics."[1]

On his own, Marconi read the scientific and technical books in the school library and subscribed to technical journals to learn about new developments. He also tried new experiments, although he lacked a real laboratory and sophisticated equipment. For one experiment, Marconi made a device with an arrow-shaped piece of zinc, then placed it on the roof of their rented house to absorb electricity from the air during storms. It was connected to a circuit that rang a bell inside the house when electricity passed through the circuit.

For his part, Giuseppe Marconi continued to criticize his son's experiments and often scolded him for being late, making a mess, or spending money for things Giuseppe considered useless and even dangerous. Yet Guglielmo Marconi felt sure he was on the right path. He later recalled that his strongest childhood memory was "the care with which I would try to hide from everybody—in order not to be teased—my irresistible feeling that one day I would be able to do something new and great."[2] As for the teachers who criticized him when he failed to study subjects that did not interest him, Marconi would tell himself, "They will realize one day . . . that I am not as dumb as they think."[3]

Although he did not know it during his school days, it was in communications that Marconi would make his mark.

During the 1800s, as he studied and experimented, communication methods were changing along with the science of electricity. Numerous scientists, including Andre Marie Ampere, Carl Gauss, and Willhelm Weber, tried to build electrical devices that would telegraph messages across long distances. In 1837, British scientists William Cooke and Charles Wheatstone created an electric needle telegraph based on Oersted's work. With their equipment, consisting of a battery that provided a constant electrical current along with copper wiring and a deflecting needle receiver, Cooke and Wheatstone were able to send messages a distance of four miles. Railway stations began using their needle telegraph to send emergency signals.

> "I would try to hide from everybody [my] feeling that one day I would do something new and great."
>
> —Guglielmo Marconi

Five years later, in 1843, American Samuel Morse patented a telegraph that relied on electromagnetism. Morse benefited from the work of other scientists, including work William Sturgeon carried out in the 1820s and research on electromagnetism that Michael Faraday and Joseph Henry conducted ten years later. Before he built the telegraph, Morse devised a code of dots and dashes to represent the letters of the alphabet. Messages using this "Morse code" were recorded on paper at the receiving station, then decoded.

People embraced telegraphy as a way to communicate over longer distances. In 1843, a forty-mile-long line was set up between Washington, D.C., and Baltimore, Maryland. The underground wires were damaged, however, and overhead wires replaced them. By 1850, the Morse telegraph was being widely used in the United States and other countries. A workable telegraph line running underwater between England and France was built in 1851, and the Atlantic telegraph cable was completed in 1866, extending about 2,700 miles from Ireland to Newfoundland. Now telegrams could be sent across the Atlantic Ocean, as well as North America. In an article praising this development, a writer for *Scientific American* said, "Our whole country has been electrified by the successful laying of the Atlantic Telegraph."[4] Some people predicted that telegraphy would even improve international relations because people could exchange thoughts and opinions more easily, and perhaps avoid political misunderstandings.

Thirty-three years later, on March 7, 1876, communications again changed dramatically when Alexander Graham Bell received a patent for the telephone. Soon, people were corresponding more often by telephone than by telegraph. Both devices were limited, however, because they required wires and other physical connections.

By 1890, thanks to his friend Nello Marchetti, Marconi had seen the telegraph in action. He devised a crude machine of his own to transmit electricity—his first Morse code transmitter. Although Marconi did not realize it at the time, a scientist named Heinrich Rudolf Hertz had recently conducted key experiments that would further open the door to the wireless.

Hertz, a professor at the Karlsruhe Polytechnic Institute in Berlin, Germany, decided to test James Maxwell's theory of electromagnetism. He wondered whether electromagnetic waves would be sent out by an electric current that flowed one way and then the other, changing direction (oscillating) very rapidly. In the past, alternating current had been known to change direction 100 to 120 times each second, which is twice its frequency. Hertz designed equipment that would make the current oscillate more rapidly than in previous experiments—thousands or millions of times each second—which produced strong, fast bursts of electricity.

Hertz's "oscillator" consisted of a high-voltage coil and a spark gap, made from bending copper wire in a loop that nearly formed a circle, with a brass ball attached to each end. He left a small gap between the adjustable brass balls where he expected to transmit electrical sparks from one ball to the other. Hertz's device could both create and detect waves, a process that was completed in just one second.

In 1888, while teaching his physics class, Hertz sent waves over a distance of several yards, using his wave detector to verify their transmission. As the electric and magnetic fields detached from the wires and crossed the small gap, Hertz proved that electricity can be transmitted in electromagnetic waves and that these waves travel in straight lines and can be reflected by a metal sheet.

Hertz went on to improve his equipment to produce larger sparks, measuring waves up to eighty centimeters long. He also timed the waves and confirmed Maxwell's hypothesis that the velocity of radio waves equals the velocity of light (which is itself a form of electromagnetic radiation). But, like Maxwell, he did not consider practical uses for this phenomenon. He told his students that although his experiments confirmed Maxwell's theory, the outcome "was of no use whatsoever."[5] Other people disagreed and began to experiment with so-called Hertzian waves (later called "radio waves"). In Italy, physicist Augusto Righi developed a new kind of oscillator to make Hertz's work more exact. His oscillator could produce longer electromagnetic waves.

Hertz might have added more insights but he died that same year, just before his thirty-seventh birthday. As a belated tribute, starting in 1933, his name was used to describe radio and electrical frequencies: hertz (Hz), kilohertz (KHz), and megahertz (MHz).

After Hertz died, more scientists examined his work. In 1891 Sir Oliver Heaviside, an English physicist and mathematician, said, "Three years ago, electromagnetic waves were nowhere. Shortly afterward, they were everywhere."[6] He added, "The great gap between Hertzian waves and light has not yet been bridged. But I have no doubt that it will be by the discovery of improved methods of generating and observing very shortwaves."[7]

Marconi was still a teenager when these momentous events took place, but he learned about Hertz's work in 1894. That summer, while his family was visiting a mountain resort in the Italian Alps, Marconi read an electrical journal called *Wiedemann's Annalen*. It contained articles commemorating Hertz, who had died earlier that year, and contained descriptions of his experiments and equipment.

After reading about Hertz's experiment, Marconi was convinced it would be possible to send signals across long distances using electromagnetic waves. He later said that he resolved at once to test "whether it would be possible by means of Hertzian waves to transmit to a distance telegraphic signs and symbols without the aid of connecting wires."[8] Despite the prevailing ideas, Marconi refused to believe that these signals must be blocked by mountains, forests, or even oceans.

If Marconi was correct, communications would obviously be transformed. During the late 1800s, people were reaping the benefits of faster communication via international telegraph and the telephone, but these devices required many miles of wires, as well as hand-operated exchanges. Ships at sea could not contact people on land. Knowing that wireless communication would solve these problems, various inventors had worked on radiotelegraphs. As a result, people would later argue about who actually "invented" the first radio.

Some men began working on wireless telegraphs before Hertz conducted his wave experiments and even before Marconi was born. One of them was Dr. Mahlon Loomis, a dentist from New York state. Loomis wrote these words in his journal on February 20, 1864: "I have been for years trying to study out a process by which telegraphic communications may be made across the ocean without any wires, and also from point to point on the earth."[9] In October 1866, Loomis held a public exhibition where he demonstrated a form of wireless communication by sending signals between two mountains, about 18 miles apart, in the Blue Ridge range of Virginia. Loomis made aerials (antennas) from kites with copper wires hanging down, and managed to make one kite cause the other to move. Two years later, sponsored by the U.S. Navy, he transmitted telegraphic signals between two ships located two miles apart on the Chesapeake Bay.

But Loomis lacked enough money to continue his work

after his backers lost money during an economic depression. His subsequent backers in Chicago were devastated by the Great Fire of 1871. When Loomis filed for a radio patent, the U.S. Congress passed a bill to create the Loomis Aerial Telegraph Company in 1873, but they failed to appropriate the funds he needed for his experiments. Although Loomis felt misunderstood and ignored, he remained certain that wireless telegraphy was possible. Before he died in 1886, he said, "The time will come when this discovery will be regarded as of more consequence to mankind than Columbus's discovery of a new world. I have not only discovered a new world, but the means of invading it."[10]

Russian scientist Alexander Stepanovitch Popov (or Popoff), also worked on radiotelegraphy. In 1896, while demonstrating for a group of scientists, Popov claimed he had repeated Hertz's experiment, sending messages by Morse code a distance of 600 yards with a wireless device. By 1898, Popov apparently had achieved transmissions of up to 3.2 km (2 miles). Russian historical sources also claimed that Popov equipped a land station and a Russian navy cruiser with his wireless equipment to create ship-to-shore communications. His wireless apparatus may have been the first ever used to help a vessel in distress. In 1900, as the battleship *General-Admiral Apraksin* was sinking in the icy Gulf of Finland with hundreds of crew aboard, they used Popov's radio system to send distress messages to land stations about 28 miles (45 km) away. These stations contacted the icebreaker *Ermak*, which went to the rescue. His homeland hailed Popov as the inventor of radio and honored him every year on May 7, and some historians call him the "Russian Marconi." Others disagree, however, and say that Russian historical sources were unreliable or that Popov's apparatus did not receive signals from other transmitters but merely recorded electrical impulses from the atmosphere, possibly resulting from storms and lightning.

At any rate, Marconi did not know about Loomis or Popov when he read about Heinrich Hertz's experiments. During his Alpine vacation, he reread the article until he knew it by heart. He could hardly wait to return home and see for himself how to create and measure Hertzian waves.

CHAPTER FOUR

"ON A GOOD ROAD"

Back home, Marconi immersed himself in materials about electricity and electromagnetic waves. He scoured the University of Bologna library for books about those topics and visited Professor Augusto Righi, the scientist who had written the journal article about Hertz. Righi agreed to let Marconi audit his physics classes at the university.

At this time, experts still claimed that wireless messages could not be sent long distances and that electromagnetic waves could only travel in a straight line—and then only if no land, water, or other objects were standing in the way. Some scientists actually demonstrated on paper that long-distance communication by wireless was impossible. It could not be done, they said, because of the curvature of the earth. Righi himself told Marconi that nobody knew how to generate enough power to create waves long enough to travel over a large distance.

Despite these discouraging predictions, Marconi thought Hertzian waves could be used to make some kind of wireless device. He later said, "I experimented with electrical waves, as I considered that line of research very interesting. . . . I thought that these waves, if produced in a somewhat different manner—that is, if they could be made more powerful, and if receivers could be made more reliable—would be applicable for telegraphing across space to great distances."[1]

Marconi needed space for new experiments, so his understanding mother convinced Giuseppe to let him use two large rooms on the top floor of the villa. Giuseppe was unhappy with this arrangement and still thought that his son was wasting time. Among other things, he complained that Marconi had not gained his secondary school diploma, which meant he could not enroll in either the Naval Academy in Leghorn or the University of Bologna.

Into the third-floor rooms of Villa Griffone, which his grandfather had once used for his silkworm business, Marconi brought books, articles, and materials. The household staff was told not to interrupt his work. Professor Righi also let Marconi use his laboratory at the University of Bologna.

As he read and thought, Marconi made diagrams of equipment he needed in order to produce signals—signals he hoped would reach beyond those in Hertz's experiments. With his long, slender fingers, he put together pieces of equipment. Although his family was prosperous, Marconi did not have much money of his own to buy materials. He used his allowance and even sold his shoes to pay for wires, batteries, and other items.

Marconi later described the equipment he developed to begin creating and testing Hertzian waves: "I constructed apparatus which was practically the same as the original Hertz apparatus for transmitting these waves. And I made a receiver which contained a detector which manifested or revealed the presence of the waves at the receiving end. . . . I had a Morse signaling key at the sending end and some kind of a detector which could be used telegraphically at the receiving end."[2]

Marconi's transmitter, consisting of an induction coil and spark gap, was battery-powered. Hertz had called it an "exciter" because it caused a spark to cross the gap between two ball electrodes. Marconi made induction coils by winding wire tightly over a soft iron core, then winding a second layer of wire over the first. As low-voltage electricity from the battery flowed through the primary wire, with periodic interruptions, it created enough voltage in the secondary wire to transmit a charge. On the spheres of the spark gap, he attached two metallic plates. The current from the battery-powered induction coil went through the telegraph key.

Practical developments in conducting materials paved the way for some of Marconi's experimental equipment. In 1866, Englishman S. A. Varley was looking for ways to protect exposed telegraph lines from lightning damage that hurt the equipment or interfered with message transmission. Through trial and error, Varley found that loosely packed tiny particles of carbon and tin clung tightly when lightning struck. He tried connecting telegraph lines to the ground using pieces of wood with hollowed out centers filled with the carbon and tin filings. These lines safely conducted electrical charges into the ground. At the time, however, Varley did not realize that his technique worked because electric waves caused the filings to stick together.

Other scientists explored this idea, sometimes using different metals. In 1878, another Englishman, David E. Hughes, found that loose filings of zinc and silver inside a Leyden jar would adhere; during the early 1880s, Italian physicist Temistocle Calzecchi-Onesti tried copper filings. Later in that decade, Professor Calzecchi-Onesti confirmed his own theory that loosely packed iron filings in a tube can conduct electricity more effectively if they are subjected to certain outside forces—for example, sparks generated by opening and closing an electrical circuit. Oliver Lodge continued that work in the 1890s, naming the tube a "coherer." Lodge's version of the coherer was later used in some wireless designs.

In France, Professor Edouard Branly developed a more sensitive coherer than his predecessors. He noticed that electromagnetic waves could affect the electrical conductivity of certain metallic particles in a glass tube. Some signals caused the particles to cohere (cling to each other). To decohere the particles, Branly tapped a tiny hammer against the tube to interrupt the current from a battery. Branly experimented with different powders, tube shapes, and positions to make his receivers more sensitive.

It was with a Branly coherer that Marconi experienced his first glimpse of success late in 1894. In fact, Marconi acknowledged that he relied on the work of other scientists as he developed his wireless. Years later, he wrote,

> By the time I was twenty, I was fairly well acquainted with the published results of the work of the most distinguished scientists who had occupied themselves with

the subject of electric waves . . . Hertz, Branly, Lodge, Righi, and many others. . . . much criticism was levelled at me in the early days because in my first experiments, I used a form of oscillator which had been devised by him and which itself was a modification of Hertz's oscillator.[3]

But, as Marconi pointed out, many famous inventors, including Thomas Edison, had also relied on theories and inventions developed by others. He noted, "I doubt very much whether there has ever been a case of a useful invention for which all the theory, all the practical applications and all the apparatus were the work of [one] man."[4]

When Marconi announced that he would keep working all winter, his mother declared that their entire family would stay at Villa Griffone, even though she felt unwell in cold weather. Marconi grew increasingly thin as he sacrificed meals, sleep, and fresh air to work in his laboratory. Though he felt discouraged at times, he continued to believe in his goal and later said, "I did not lose courage."[5]

A breakthrough moment occurred one night in December 1894. Marconi managed to send radio waves nine yards across the room in his home laboratory. When he pressed the switch on his transmitter, a bell rang. Clearly, electromagnetic waves produced this effect. He was so excited that he ran to awaken his mother, always his staunchest supporter, and took her up to the attic to witness his achievement.

After this promising event, Marconi set out to transmit waves across longer distances. He moved his experiments outside to the grounds and gardens of the villa, where he had more space to try sending messages across longer distances. His father remained skeptical and complained about the trail of coils, tubes, wires, and poles in the garden. Yet he realized that his son had achieved some results and agreed to give him small amounts of money for equipment. The twenty-two-year-old Marconi also had some help from his brother Alfonso and two men who worked at the villa: a young tenant farmer named Mignani and a carpenter named Vornelli.

Later, in his Nobel Prize address, Marconi described the insights that helped him progress during the early months of 1895: "After a few preliminary experiments with Hertzian waves I became very soon convinced, that if these waves or similar waves could be reliably transmitted and received over considerable distances a new system of communication would become available possessing enormous advantages over flashlights and optical methods, which are so much dependent for their success on the clearness of the atmosphere."[6]

He knew that he must improve his equipment in order to send and detect radio waves (Hertzian waves) from greater distances. The Branly coherer was not reliable enough for more advanced work, so he explored other ways to assemble a coherer, and his improvements made a crucial difference. By placing a mixture of about 95 percent nickel and 5 percent silver filings in a small gap between two silver plugs in a tube, he devised a coherer that was more reliable and sensitive than his previous model. It was painstaking work, because the best results came when the filings were extremely fine and consistent in size. He later said that he then placed the coherer in a circuit "containing a voltaic cell and sensitive telegraph relay actuating another circuit, which worked a tapper or trembler and a recording

An illustration showing a young Marconi working with some of his earliest radio equipment.

instrument."[7] This mechanism would allow him to transmit messages about a mile.

Marconi also developed more efficient antennas that helped him to send signals across longer distances. His innovative method of connecting his transmitter and receiver to the ground, called a "ground return," enabled Marconi to succeed where others had failed. The aerial circuit on Marconi's transmitter was connected on one end to an elevated aerial, with the other end connected to the ground. He later explained, "In August 1895, I discovered a new arrangement which not only greatly increased the distance over which I could communicate, but also seemed to make the transmission independent from the effects of intervening obstacles. This arrangement consisted in connecting one terminal of the Hertzian oscillator, or spark producer, to earth and the other terminal to a wire or capacity area placed at a height above the ground, and in also connecting at the receiving end one terminal of the coherer to the earth and the other to an elevated conductor."[8]

When a low-frequency current moved through the spark gap, it produced high-frequency oscillations, which were radiated by the aerial. The signals Marconi was sending became much stronger once he arranged one metal slab high above the ground while leaving the other on the ground. He later wrote, "I understood in that moment that I was on a good road. My invention had taken life. I had made an important discovery."[9]

While they worked outside, Marconi and his helpers communicated with a Morse code transmitter that included a sending key and receiver that worked a buzzer. They signaled each other using dots and dashes. When Alfonso received one of Guglielmo's messages, he would wave a handkerchief to show the message arrived.

When Marconi achieved his next breakthrough in late September 1895, even his father was impressed. In this new experiment, Alfonso, Mignani, and Vornelli placed the receiver about 1.86 miles (3 km) away, behind a hill, while Marconi remained near the house with his transmitter. Since he could not see the others, they had arranged beforehand to fire a rifle shot if any signals arrived. Once Marconi was sure the receiver was in place, he began tapping out the three dots of the letter "S" in Morse code. He later recalled, "In the distance a shot echoed down the valley."[10] That all-important gunshot showed Marconi that his message had arrived! Clearly, this was a significant achievement, because the message had traveled over a hill, where the receiver was not in sight.

By early 1896, Marconi was sending messages over a mile. Giuseppe now believed in his son's work and agreed to provide more funds for his research effort. With his family's advice and encouragement, Marconi prepared to tell other people about radiotelegraphy. He would need official recognition, as well as more money, in order to develop his promising invention.

CHAPTER FIVE

PATENTS AND PROMOTIONS

Convinced that his invention was important, Marconi decided to inform the Italian government and ask for their support. With the help of some trusted community leaders, the Marconi family wrote a letter to the Italian Ministry of Post and Telegraph. In the letter, he suggested that the government might find ways to use his wireless and could help him develop it.

The government wrote back and declined his request. Signor Sineo, the Italian minister of Post and Telegraph, said that Marconi's device was "not suitable for telecommunications."[1] He commented, "Our telegraph works. Why do we need a wireless telegraph?"[2]

A disappointed Marconi then decided to approach Britain, the world's leading maritime nation. He later explained, "I offered wireless telegraphy to Italy, but it was intimated to me that perhaps, in view of the close connection between wireless telegraphy and the sea, it would be better to go to England, where the maritime activities are more highly developed and, after all, it was logically the best country for my first attempts at overseas signalling."[3]

Annie Marconi had important connections in England. She began writing to relatives and friends, including an uncle who was a colonel in the British army. One of their friends in Bologna, Dr. Gardini, wrote a letter of introduction to the Italian ambassador in London, informing him that Marconi "has succeeded in sending signals by means of the wireless telegraph a distance of one thousand five hundred meters with a machine he has invented."[4] The family agreed that Annie would accompany her son to London in order to meet with the people who could help them. In the meantime, Marconi did not show his experiments to other scientists. He wanted to wait until he obtained legal patents that would protect the invention and help him profit from his work.

In February 1896, Marconi and his mother set out for England with high hopes, but encountered problems when they reached British soil. A customs inspector feared that Marconi's unusual-looking equipment might be some kind of weapon, so he took the transmitter apart. In the process, he damaged Marconi's equipment. Now Marconi would need to buy new parts and make repairs before he could show anybody his wireless.

When they arrived in London, the Marconis were happy to see Henry Jameson-Davis waiting for them at the train station. Jameson-Davis, who was Annie's nephew and Marconi's cousin, helped them settle into a relative's home until they could rent their own home in London. As a trained engineer, he could discuss Marconi's work and help him repair his broken transmitter. Next, he introduced

Marconi to a lawyer who specialized in patent law, and they began writing the papers they must file to protect his invention. A government patent meant official recognition for the inventor, and it banned other people from copying the invention without permission.

Another Jameson family friend provided more help. William Preece, the Engineer-in-Chief at the General Post Office in London, was excited about Marconi's wireless and asked some British officials to attend a demonstration. He also found him an assistant: George Stephen Kemp, who became Marconi's friend and continued to serve as his chief assistant until he died in 1933. Together they worked to improve the original wireless.

That spring, Marconi impressed onlookers when he projected beam-like waves across a distance of 100 yards. Then, in September 1896, during a demonstration for British officials, he transmitted messages 1.75 miles (2.8 km). People were starting to hear about Marconi's invention, and some scientists began speculating about how the wireless worked.

Marconi himself focused on developing stronger, more efficient equipment. From the moment he began working on his wireless, Marconi had believed he could find ways to send messages across significant distances. To achieve that goal, he knew the wireless would need more sensitive and stable equipment—coherer, detector, amplifiers, and oscillators.

Ordinarily, a young man his age would be drafted into the military, but the Italian government let Marconi work instead at the Italian Embassy in London. As a result, once he fulfilled his assigned duties, he could spend the rest of his time on his experiments. Since Marconi received money from his father back in Italy, he anonymously donated his embassy paychecks to the Italian Hospital in Bloomsbury, London.

While Marconi worked at the embassy and promoted his invention, he found that he could improve his wireless by using a tuner. He later explained how he tried to adjust the tuning of his early apparatus by cutting off part of the wire: "My antenna in 1896, varied from six to thirty to forty feet. If I wanted to change the period [tuning] I let the antenna down and cut if off at the bottom. I first used an inductance coil [tuner] in the antenna about the end of 1898."[5]

Advances in physics and aid from the British government helped him to move forward. In 1897, British physicist J. J. Thomson discovered the electron—a miniscule part of the atom that has a negative charge. His finding would revolutionize wireless communication, as well as lead to new developments for the telephone, radio, and computer science.

That same year, the British Ministry of Posts provided money and technicians for Marconi's experiments. Steadily, he and his team found ways to increase the distances for his wireless transmissions—from five kilometers to eight, fifteen, thirty, and eventually 100 kilometers.

For the next few years, Marconi and his staff would seek ways to tune the transmitter and receiver to more precise frequencies. Frequency refers to the number of waves per second, and, as frequency increases, wavelength decreases. When two or more transmitters sent out radio signals at the same time and place, receivers picked up a confusing mixture of sounds were picked up by receivers. Marconi knew he must adjust the electrical circuits of his transmitter and receiver to a narrow range of frequencies.

In June 1897, the Italian government finally showed an interest in his invention. An Italian naval captain stationed in London had been observing Marconi's experiments, including a successful transmission across England's Bristol Channel, conducted in bad weather. After hearing these reports, Italian officials asked Marconi to demonstrate his wireless for them.

Marconi was glad to accept, not only because he was returning in triumph but also because he missed Italy. When he arrived, Marconi performed a demonstration for the navy, sending out the words "Viva l'Italia" in Morse code. He repeated the demonstration for King Humberto I and Queen Margharita, and the Italian ministers, members of Parliament, and scientists they had invited to watch. Yet, the scientific community remained skeptical about Marconi's work, claiming that he had not yet transmitted signals across long distances.

The Italian government offered Marconi the money and equipment he needed to test his wireless at sea. He proceeded to carry out new tests at La Spezia, using equipment like that he had used in the Bristol Channel, and operating under varied weather conditions. Admiral Ernest Simion, who watched the tests, later wrote, "These experiments . . . which were the first with the receiver on board ship, showed beyond dispute the value that the system could have for the Navy."[6]

Meanwhile, back in England, William Preece conducted new tests at the coastal town of Dover to prepare for their new test—sending messages across the English Channel from England to France. Marconi's work was now attracting support from influential people, including the famous physicist William Thomson (Lord Kelvin), who encouraged him to continue.

While developing and promoting his invention, Marconi continued to manage his business affairs. He had taken care to protect his work, and the profits he expected to earn, since he arrived in England. In 1896, he received his first patent—No. 12039, issued for the use of a transmitter and the coherer connected to the earth and the elevated antenna. The American equivalent of this patent was issued the following year.

Then, in July 1897, he authorized his cousin Henry Jameson-Davis to form the Wireless Telegraph & Signal Company, Ltd., in London. The company owned Marconi's patents, along with the rights to develop, market, and sell his inventions around the world. However, Marconi imposed no legal restrictions on his homeland and permitted Italy to use or develop radio equipment without regard to his patents.

After Marconi returned from Italy, he completed the negotiations to form his new company. In return for his patent rights, he was given £ 15,000 in cash. Because he also owned a controlling majority of the shares of stock in the company, other investors could help to set the policies, but Marconi retained a great deal of control.

He was disappointed, however, that the company did not bear his name. This was especially important to his father, who had expressed his wishes to his son verbally and in writing. On July 7, he wrote urging Marconi to make sure his attorney handled this matter, saying, "the Italian government would like your discovery [to be] developed under your name. It seems that, on the contrary, the English company plans not to use it. . . . the new company should bear your name."[7]

In time, they would get their wish. The name was officially changed from the Wireless Telegraph & Signal Company, Ltd., to the Marconi Wireless Telegraph Company Ltd., in 1900.

As Marconi dealt with various scientific and business affairs, his invention was already being put to use. Both the British and Italian governments now realized the wireless could facilitate communication at sea. On Britain's Isle of Wight, a radio station featuring radio antennas over 100 feet tall was set up at Alum Bay. Residents were intrigued by the sight of tall antennas and kites lifting wires high in the air. Although scientists predicted that wind or severe weather could block radio waves, Marconi thought he could overcome these problems.

In 1898, Marconi installed a radio aboard the Royal Yacht Osborne. While Albert, the Prince of Wales, sailed around the Isle of Wight, Marconi conducted various experiments as the prince exchanged more than 150 messages with his mother, Queen Victoria. When the voyage ended after sixteen days, the queen congratulated Marconi and wished him continuing success.

That same year, his company also set up a radio system on the north coast of Ireland, with one lighthouse station on Rathlin Island and another at Ballycastle. In July, the Irish *Dublin Express* produced the first news report based on radioed information, sent to them by Marconi himself.

Riding in a tugboat, he watched yachts racing in the Irish Sea during the Kingstown Regatta, then telephoned the results to Dublin. This event showed more people how the wireless could change their lives.

The sea-loving Marconi was delighted when the military began using his wireless on warships and some steamships. He was even more thrilled when his invention began saving lives. On March 3, 1899, when a steamship became trapped off the shore of Dover, radio operators at the East Goodwin lightship sent messages to the mainland. The lifeboats they sent to the site were able to retrieve all the crew and most of the valuable cargo on board. These events showed more people that radiotelegraphy was quite practical, not just an interesting "toy."

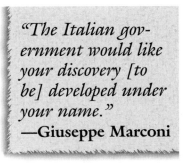

"The Italian government would like your discovery [to be] developed under your name."
—**Giuseppe Marconi**

In 1899, the U.S. Army set up a lightship off Fire Island, New York, with wireless communication, and the U.S. Navy adopted a wireless system in 1901. That same year, radiotelegraph service was installed among five Hawaiian islands. Marconi's company also installed wireless transmitters for the navies of Britain, Italy, and Germany, and expanded its business contacts with shipping lines around the world.

As news of the wireless grew, people were curious to see if signals could move across the English Channel. In 1899, Marconi had a chance to find out. He had already set up a radiotelegraph station on the English coast at South Foreland when the French government agreed that he could install a station in Wimereux, thirty-two miles across the

Channel to France. This village was located near Boulogne, where his parents had been married thirty-five years earlier.

On March 27, Marconi was ready in a room at the Chalet d'Artois in France, while his fellow operator in South Foreland prepared for the flurry of messages they would soon exchange. After successfully sending a message with the letter "V" (for "victory" in the struggle for long-distance communication), Marconi proceeded to transmit and receive more messages, including one that paid tribute to Frenchman Edouard Branly, for his work on the coherer.

Marconi had achieved the first international radiotele-graph connection, a feat that brought him increased recognition. He later described it as "the most important thing I did."[8]

But there was much more to accomplish. Despite formidable obstacles and the doubts expressed by most scientists, Marconi planned to transmit signals across the Atlantic Ocean.

CHAPTER SIX

ACROSS THE OCEAN

By 1900, communication technology had taken some giant leaps forward. The number of telephones in the United States reached 1 million. The international telegraph network was in place, and, in Great Britain alone, about 400 million telegrams were sent that year. Marconi had transmitted wireless signals across the English Channel. What lay ahead for this exciting new form of communication?

Marconi looked forward to installing the wireless in more locations and making it even more useful. In addition, he hoped to silence many critics by sending signals across the Atlantic Ocean. He did not, however, openly discuss this plan, because, as he explained in 1902, "I was not desirous of entering upon a discussion of the subject until I could satisfy myself by experiments that it could be accomplished."[1]

While looking ahead, Marconi had business decisions to make, and he was invited to visit Australia, China, Brazil, and other places, where he promoted his wireless. His daughter Degna later wrote, "There were three tasks of major import which confronted Father as 1900 opened: to keep abreast of the paperwork of his expanding company; to prepare for tests preliminary to the next great leap across space—spanning the Atlantic; and to bring his latest work to the point where he could patent it."[2]

The Wireless Telegraph & Signal Company itself began the new century in deep financial trouble. Though their equipment was becoming more widely known, the cost of running the business and funding new research and technology exceeded their income. Unless profits increased quickly, they could be forced to shut down. At one point, Marconi borrowed more than fifty thousand pounds from England's largest banks to stay afloat.

Positive changes began to occur in February 1900, after the board of directors decided to rename the company "Marconi's Wireless Telegraph Company, Ltd." Marconi had not suggested this change himself but was pleased with the decision. Shortly thereafter, the company's stock rose in value from $3 to $22 per share. New investors included American industrial giant Andrew Carnegie and inventor Thomas Edison, who became a consulting engineer to Marconi's American branch.

Business also picked up as the company gained more lucrative contracts. At the request of the German government, Marconi's company sent George Kemp to Bremen to install wireless equipment on the SS *Kaiser Wilhelm*. That April, the company formed a division called Marconi International Marine Communication Company, with main offices located in London and Brussels and agencies in Paris and Rome. Marconi himself served as one of its fourteen directors, representing seven countries. This new division took its first big order early in July when the British admiralty requested 32 wireless sets, for which they agreed to pay royalties of £ 100 a year.

After the marine division demonstrated its wireless system to Belgian officials, the company received a contract to set up a station on shore to send and receive messages with Belgian mail boats carrying cargo to Dover, England. Before the year was out, Britain and Ireland would place more orders.

In the meantime, Marconi and his team prepared for their next big feat—transatlantic transmission. To meet this challenge, Marconi knew he must improve his equipment and develop new devices that would allow long-range transmission. Long-wave signals required far more power than short-wave signals, so Marconi aimed to produce a more powerful spark at least two inches long. In addition, he realized, as he said in 1909, that "it was also necessary to increase the area or height of the transmitting and receiving elevated conductors."[3]

During the late 1890s, Marconi had recruited physicists and engineers with the skills and vision he needed to develop more sophisticated technology. One of them, John Ambrose Fleming, had been a professor of electrical technology at University College in London before he joined Marconi's company in 1899 as a consultant. Marconi's colleague, Richard Norman Vyvyan, later described Fleming's contribution:

> To get signals across the Atlantic, Marconi had calculated that he would require a capacity of 1/50th of a microfarad [a unit of capacitance equal to one-millionth of a

farad] discharging across a two-inch spark gap. One of the many problems was to obtain this by the single action of a transformer on a condenser without raising the transformer voltage to an unworkable value. Dr. Fleming thereupon devised a method of double transformation, whereby the current from a transformer was employed to charge a condenser, discharging through an oscillation transformer across a spark gap. The secondary of the transformer, consisting of more turns that the primary, was connected to a second spark gap, a second condenser and the primary winding of a second oscillation transformer being also across this spark gap. The secondary of the last transformer was in series with the aerial.[4]

With this double transformer system, electrical power was increased, and then increased still more, in order to bring extremely high voltage to the aerial.

In April 1900, just one day after his maritime division was formed, Marconi obtained an important new patent for a system that reduced the problem of mutual interference in wireless transmissions. His method for "selective tuning" involved tuning the circuits in the transmitter, receiver, and aerial to the same wavelength. Selective tuning offered huge benefits for wireless at sea, especially as power was extended to longer ranges. Without selective tuning, when ships and/or stations on shore sent messages at the same time, the result was overlap and mutual interference. Patent 7777 helped to solve that problem.

The inspiration for selective tuning came from experiments that Professor Oliver Lodge had conducted on tuning sending and receiving aerials in 1897. Years later, Lodge filed a lawsuit over the 7777 patent. For now,

Marconi and his colleagues had another tool that would help them conduct the transatlantic project.

Attempting to transmit across the Atlantic involved vast investments of time and money—about $2.75 million in today's figures. The Marconi Company's Board of Directors was wary of taking this chance, because experts thought the curvature of the earth would prevent success. Marconi argued that previous tests had shown waves could travel beyond the horizon, so that meant they could cross the Atlantic. Once the board agreed, he began looking for the best locations on both sides of the ocean to conduct the test. In July, while inspecting sites in Cornwall on England's southwestern coast, Marconi chose a site at Poldhu.

That October, workers began constructing a station according to the design John Ambrose Fleming had created. It called for an oil engine that would drive an alternator linked to twenty high wooden masts, 200-feet (60 m) high, arranged in a ring with a diameter of 200 feet. Marconi and his crew spent eleven months erecting their most powerful radio station yet, able to send signals at least one hundred times more powerful than any of their previous stations.

The plant was ready for the first tests in January 1901, and Marconi was encouraged when he succeeded in sending some preliminary signals. By spring, the station was completely done and a receiving station was set up at Cape Cod, on the Massachusetts' coast of the United States. But setbacks occurred, in the form of severe weather that toppled the large aerials on both continents. In September, after winds struck the aerial in Poldhu, it had to be replaced.

In November, a storm destroyed the masts and antennae at the Cape Cod station.

Instead of Cape Cod, Marconi and his team decided to transmit to a different site, Newfoundland, which was located over 2,000 miles away from Poldhu. Marconi traveled by ship to St. John's, on the eastern coast of Newfoundland, to set up a temporary receiving station. Once they arrived, Marconi and his assistants George Kemp and G. W. Paget unloaded their cargo of balloons and large kites. Knowing that it would be extremely difficult to build workable towers on Newfoundland's stormy, windswept coast, Marconi had decided to use balloons or kites to support an aerial. He also met with government officials who offered to assist his work, though they believed he was merely carrying out more wireless tests on ships at sea.

Marconi later wrote, "After taking a look at several sites which might prove suitable, I considered that the best one was to be found on Signal Hill, a lofty eminence overlooking the port and forming the natural bulwark which protects it from the fury of the Atlantic gales."[5] Signal Hill lay across the bay from St. John's. From there, Marconi attempted to send a ten-pound aerial up by attaching it to a balloon that contained 1,000 cubic feet of hydrogen gas, but it broke off and was blown out to sea.

The next day, he tried again, this time with a kite, which a high wind carried up 400 feet into the air. Paget later recalled, "It flew over the stormy Atlantic, surged up and down by the gale tugging at its six hundred foot aerial wire. The icy rain lashed my face as I watched it anxiously. The wind howled around the building where, in a small dark room furnished with a table, one chair and some packing cases, Mr. Kemp sat at the receiving set while Mr. Marconi drank a cup of cocoa before taking his turn at listening for the signals which were being transmitted from Poldhu, at least we hoped so."[6]

That great moment would finally arrive on December 12, 1901. According to the plan Marconi had made in England, the station at Poldhu was supposed to send out signals every day from 12 noon to 3 P.M., St. John's time. For these tests, they chose the letter "S," which is formed in Morse code by making three dots. Marconi sat in a shack on a cliff, waiting. He could not tune in to the signals, which were supposed to be sent consistently, because the wave meter had not yet been invented. He later recalled the events leading up to the moment that would make history:

> It was shortly after mid-day (local time) on 12 December 1901, that I placed a single ear-phone to my ear and started listening. The receiver on the table before me was very crude—a few coils and condensers and a coherer, no valves, no amplifier, not even a crystal. I was at last on the point of putting the correctness of all my beliefs to the test.[7]

Although he listened closely, Marconi did not hear anything at first. Then, suddenly, a sound came into the receiver . . . first a sharp click of the tapper, which meant something was coming . . . then three clicks, very faint . . . but they continued to arrive. Excited but cautious, Marconi wanted someone else to verify what he was hearing, so he handed the telephone to Kemp, who said that he, too, could hear the signals. They had transmitted across the Atlantic Ocean!

Throughout the afternoon, they heard the letter S several

more times, but weather conditions affected the kite, which prevented them from hearing signals consistently. Still, Marconi felt sure they had succeeded. After he detected signals three days in a row, he was ready to announce this momentous event to the Marconi Company officials and then to the press.

Newspapers around the world spread the news. The front page of the *New York Times* headlined the story on December 14, 1901, with the words "Wireless Spans the Ocean."[8] They wrote "Guglielmo Marconi announced tonight the most wonderful scientific development of recent times."[9] At the young age of twenty-seven, he was about to become famous.

As the news spread, Marconi received thousands of telegrams from around the world. People expressed delight, but also shock and skepticism when they heard the news. Even some of Marconi's supporters wondered if the signals he heard might have come from somewhere else, not the transmitter thousands of miles away. Telephone inventor Alexander Graham Bell declared, "I doubt Marconi did that. It's an impossibility."[10]

Yet Thomas Edison admitted the possibility, saying, "I am astonished. I would like to meet this young man who had the monumental audacity to attempt and to succeed in jumping an electrical wave clear across the Atlantic Ocean."[11] And *The New York Times* continued to support Marconi's claim. In an article that appeared on December 17, a *Times* reporter wrote:

> If Marconi succeeds in his experiments with intercontinental wireless telegraphy, his name will stand through the ages among the very first of the world's greatest

IN THIS 1901 PHOTO, MARCONI READS SIGNALS ON A TAPE RECORDER (LEFT) WITH A TEN-INCH SPARK COIL THAT WAS USED FOR SHIP-TO-SHORE RADIO TESTS.

inventors. The thing he is attempting to do would be almost transforming in its effect upon the special life, the business and political relations of the peoples of the earth.[12]

Some people speculated about the scientific aspects of the test. They said that if the waves were electrical waves, they would travel in straight lines out into space, but this transatlantic transmission made it clear they did not. How had the electromagnetic wave traveled over the curve of the Atlantic Ocean at about the same speed as light? At the time, scientists could not explain this wonder.

Twenty years later, this was explained when British physicist Edward Appleton found out about the ionosphere, a layer of ionized gas particles produced by the sun's radiation that surrounds the earth at a height of about 100 miles. This electrified layer in the upper atmosphere reflects radio waves back to earth, in effect bouncing them back to earth where they then rebound again to the ionosphere. This process is repeated until the radiating wave loses all its energy.

Scientists later wondered what wavelength Marconi had used for the transatlantic signal, especially because the signal had been detected at around noon. At that time of day, the sun is high in the sky, and the sun absorbs most of the strength of electromagnetic waves. In 1935, Sir Ambrose Fleming said that the wavelength had not been measured during the 1901 experiment, because he had not invented his wavemeter until 1904. Fleming said, "My estimate was that the original wavelength must have been not less than about 3,000 feet (approximately 1,000 meters) but it was considerably lengthened later on."[13]

Although the scientific details were not yet known immediately after Marconi's great transatlantic test, the implications were enormous. Wireless held great commercial and practical possibilities, and the man who developed it was on the brink of more fame, along with wealth and great changes in his personal life.

CHAPTER SEVEN

FAME AND FAMILY

On the evening of January 13, about 300 invited guests came to dine at the Astor Gallery of New York's Waldorf Astoria Hotel, while crowds of other people filled the balconies. They had come to honor Guglielmo Marconi at a banquet sponsored by the American Institute of Electrical Engineers (AIEE). A board posted on the wall behind the head table symbolized Marconi's transatlantic success. It held the word "Poldhu" on one end and "St. John's" on the other, connected by a silken cord with lights that blinked out the Morse code letter "S."

Marconi, who sat at the head table with such scientific stars as Charles P. Steinmetz, Alexander Graham Bell, and Elihu Thomson, rose to accept an enthusiastic ovation. The toastmaster then read numerous letters praising his transatlantic victory, including messages from Thomas Edison and Nikola Tesla. During his own speech, Marconi thanked the various scientists, past and present, whose work had laid the groundwork for his wireless, and he praised the scientists and other people who had been working with him.

After weeks of hard work and public appearances, Marconi was ready to return to England. He was tired and eager to see his mother, about whom he said, "She's the only person on earth who understood my misgivings and trepidation when I left for Newfoundland."[1] After a brief visit, however, Marconi left once again for North America to continue his work.

More hurdles lay before him. Marconi had to negotiate an agreement with the Canadian government that would give him the legal right to continue operating the station he had set up in Nova Scotia for the transatlantic test. He also was eager to activate the installation at Cape Cod.

Besides, he had more scientific questions to answer. Now that he knew wireless could span the Atlantic, Marconi believed that it could eventually circle the earth. To prove that the rotation of the earth would not affect the passage of electrical waves, he planned to send west-to-east messages from a ship while he was crossing the Atlantic.

At the end of February 1902, Marconi sailed back to the United States on the SS *Philadelphia*. During the trip, he recorded signals sent from the Poldhu station at distances ranging from 250 miles to 2,099 miles. The crew and passengers on the ship were able to witness these transmissions as they occurred. When he arrived in New York, Marconi showed yards of tape, filled with dots and dashes, to reporters. He was pleased to give them concrete evidence that wireless could transmit messages across the Atlantic. Some people, including scientists, thought he might have heard something else, possibly due to the presence of a ship containing a wireless. Oliver Lodge expressed his doubts in a letter to *The New York Times*, in which he wrote, "Proof is, of course, still absent." He went on to say, "but . . . Marconi has awakened sympathy and a hope that his energy and enterprise may not have been deceived by unwanted electrical dryness of what wintry shore."[2]

This kind of skepticism continued to dwindle after Marconi and his team succeeded in sending messages in the form of complete sentences to Poldhu from stations in Nova Scotia, and later from Cape Cod, on the Massachusetts shore. During the summer of 1902, the Italian navy agreed to put a ship at Marconi's disposal so that he could operate from a "floating laboratory." Under his direction, Luigi Solari and their staff conducted experiments between different ships and between ship and shore.

On January 19, 1903, the official American Marconi station was opened on Cape Cod. The first messages were greetings exchanged by Britain's King Edward VII and U.S. President Theodore Roosevelt.

While Marconi forged ahead, competition was brewing. That same year, some American companies and a German company called Telefunken entered the wireless business. Marconi tried to dominate the business by ordering Marconi operators not to communicate with any ships or stations that were supplied by other manufacturers.

Along with competition from other companies, Marconi faced legal challenges to his patents. Some major improvements in wireless had evolved from a patent he acquired in 1900, his famous patent #7777 for "Improvements in Apparatus for Wireless Telegraphy"—namely, tuned or syntonic telegraphy. With electronics expert John Ambrose Fleming, Marconi had developed this four-circuit tuner to reduce interference when two or more stations operated at the same time. This apparatus could send and receive many messages of more than one frequency with a single aerial.

Between 1902 and 1912, Marconi's company received several new patents for inventions. One of the 1902 patents was issued for his magnetic detector, which was used as the standard wireless receiver for many years. Three years later, Marconi patented his horizontal directional aerial. These devices made the wireless even more useful, especially at sea.

After 1901, companies and individuals began to challenge patent #7777 and some of Marconi's other patents. His company faced legal challenges from Telefunken in Germany and from Nikola Tesla, a Serbian-American inventor, engineer, and scientist. In 1897, Tesla had filed his own radio patent applications, numbered 645,576 and 649,621, and the U.S. Patent Office granted them in 1900. When Marconi filed for his patent in 1900, the U.S. Patent Office initially turned him down, saying that Tesla had precedence. In 1901, after Marconi achieved his transatlantic feat, Otis Pond, an engineer working for Tesla, said, "Looks as if Marconi got the jump on you." Tesla replied, "Marconi is a good fellow. Let him continue. He is using seventeen of my patents."[3]

Then, in 1904, the U.S. Patent Office reversed its previous decisions and granted Marconi a patent for the invention of radio. This set the stage for various legal actions in the years to come, not only with Tesla, but also with other people. One long-running conflict involved the American inventor Lee de Forest. Dr. de Forest developed a triode valve, which increased wireless amplification. Marconi's scientific advisor Ambrose Fleming called the triode a variation of their patented diode valve. When Marconi challenged de Forest in court, he won his case but the legal fees caused a financial setback for his company, which was already straining from the cost of operating the stations in Glace Bay and Clifden.

Cash flow was poor during 1907 and 1908. By the end of 1907, the company had accumulated a debt of over £ 93,000, about £ 5 million in today's currency. To keep the company afloat, Marconi had to pledge his own funds as collateral, and they had to discharge 150 employees.

While Marconi's company was on the brink of financial collapse, his wireless was proving itself to be ever more useful. By 1902, seventy ships were equipped with wireless, and the ships' operators could contact twenty-five different land stations to request information or emergency help.

More than one company now was providing wireless equipment and operators, so people began looking for uniform ways to send and receive messages. In 1903, nine nations sent representatives to a conference in Berlin to discuss some international standards. They agreed that the three-letter code "SOS" would be the internationally recognized signal for "distress." They also agreed that any shore station in their respective nations would handle messages sent to or from any ship at sea, no matter which company had made the equipment they were using. Out of loyalty to Marconi and his company, however, England and Italy refused to sign this agreement.

The quest for international standards continued. When another conference was held three years later, the newly formed Bureau of International Telegraph Union adopted world-wide frequency allocations and regulations.

Marconi offered to lease British-made equipment to the U.S. Navy, but they refused because he insisted on a long-term contract and royalties. They also did not want to sign a contract saying that messages could be relayed only from Marconi-equipped ships. The Navy proceeded to buy a system called the Slaby-Arco from Germany's Telefunken. In 1904, they put this equipment on twenty-four naval vessels and in twenty coastal stations. Merchant ships were predominantly equipped with Marconi devices, however, and, by 1909, most U.S. coastal stations were, too.

While his business experienced ups and downs, Marconi's personal life was also changing. Through the years, he had been romantically involved with several women. At least two of these relationships almost led to marriage before they decided to end their engagement. As Marconi reached age thirty, he thought more about marriage and children. His own father died in March 1904. Giuseppe Marconi had lived long enough to see his son's business flourish, but not long enough to see him with a family of his own.

In late summer 1904, while visiting friends in England, Marconi met nineteen-year-old Beatrice O'Brien. She was one of fourteen children born to an Irish baron and his wife, and she had grown up among royalty and other prominent people. High-spirited "Bea" was reared mostly in the country and could ride and sail well. Marconi was smitten at their first meeting, and began to court this lively girl with sparkling dark eyes and thick wavy hair. A few weeks later, he asked her to marry him, but she refused.

Le Petit Journal

Le Petit Journal	5 CENTIMES SUPPLÉMENT ILLUSTRÉ 5 CENTIMES	ABONNEMENTS

CHAQUE JOUR — 8 PAGES — 5 CENTIMES

Administration : 61, rue Lafayette

Le Supplément illustré

CHAQUE SEMAINE 5 CENTIMES

Le Petit Journal Militaire, Maritime, Colonial.... 10 cent.
Le Petit Journal agricole, 5 cent. ~ La Mode du Petit Journal, 10 cent.
Le Petit Journal illustré de la Jeunesse, 10 cent.

On s'abonne sans frais dans tous les bureaux de poste

SIX MOIS   UN AN
SEINE et SEINE-ET-OISE.. 2 fr.   3 fr. 50
DÉPARTEMENTS......... 2 fr.   4 fr. »
ÉTRANGER .... 2 50   5 fr. »

Les manuscrits ne sont pas rendus

Dix-huitième Année   DIMANCHE 24 NOVEMBRE 1907   Numéro 888

THE FRONT PAGE OF *LA PETIT JOURNAL* ON NOVEMBER 24, 1907, WITH ILLUSTRATIONS OF EDOUARD BRANLY (UPPER LEFT) AND MARCONI (LOWER RIGHT). THE STORY FOLLOWED THE PROGRESS OF WIRELESS TRANSMISSIONS, WHICH HAD JUST BEEN SUCCESSFULLY MADE BETWEEN PARIS, FRANCE, AND CASABLANCA, IN NORTH AFRICA.

Disappointed, Marconi embarked on a trip to the Balkans but he did not forget about Beatrice. When they met again, he resumed courting her, and this time she accepted his proposal. In late December, she wrote to her sister, "We got engaged on the nineteenth and I never slept a wink till five in the morning. My feelings have been so extraordinary and wild I haven't been able to write, though I tried hard. . . . and to think I never meant to marry!"[4]

On March 16, 1905, the couple was married in an Anglican service. Many uninvited members of the public lined the streets to see Marconi and his new bride, along with the prominent guests who were invited to St. George's Church, which was the most fashionable in London. The *Daily Mirror* newspaper reported, "Today's wedding is not only the wedding of the week but one of the weddings of the season, for it is that of Miss Beatrice O'Brien, daughter of Ellen Lady Inchiquin, to the Chevalier Marconi, whose fame is world-wide."[5]

After their brief honeymoon at an Irish castle, Marconi had to leave for London on business. His new bride soon found herself living in remote parts of Nova Scotia and Ireland while her husband conducted experiments and worked to improve his stations. Guglielmo and Beatrice would eventually have four children together. Their first-born, Lucia, died a few weeks after birth. Daughter Degna was born in 1908; a son, Giulio, arrived in 1910; and another daughter, Gioia, was born in 1916.

As Marconi's family began to grow, wireless continued to expand its horizons. In 1905, wireless reported the naval battle of Port Arthur in the Russo-Japanese War. Two years later, the Marconi company opened the first commercial transatlantic service, between Glace Bay, Nova Scotia, and Clifden, Ireland. A public radio service spanning a shorter distance already had been set up in Italy between Bari and Avidari in Montenegro. Then, in 1909, newspapers reported the exciting news that explorer Robert E. Peary had radio-telegraphed his announcement: "I found the North Pole."[6]

Wireless was relatively new when some maritime disasters showed its value, thus spurring its growth. On January 23, 1909, the passenger ship SS *Republic* was traveling from New York City toward the Mediterranean Sea when it collided with an Italian freighter, the SS *Florida*, in dense fog off the coast of Nantucket. The *Florida* had no wireless, but the *Republic* was equipped, and its operator sent out distress signals. Within thirty minutes, a rescue ship arrived to save 1,650 passengers. As a result, the loss of life was much lower than it might have been—only two passengers and four seamen from the *Florida* perished, all at the time of impact.

The growing number of stations meant that more skilled operators were needed, too. The Marconi Wireless Telegraph Company had set up its first two schools for wireless telegraph operators in England in 1901, and the school in Essex eventually became known as Marconi College after it was moved to Chelmsford. Another school was set up in 1912, offering a six-week course to about sixty students at a time. To accommodate even more students, Marconi schools were founded in Madrid, Spain, and in New York City.

The practical uses of wireless at sea helped to bring Marconi the coveted Nobel Prize in 1909. The announcement was not only a personal triumph, but also a cause for celebration in his native land, because Marconi was the first Italian to receive a Nobel prize for physics. (Nearly three decades later, in 1938, nuclear physicist Enrico Fermi became the second.)

Marconi and his wife Beatrice traveled to Sweden by train, accompanied by her sister Lilah. This marked a happy occasion for the couple, who had experienced some problems since their marriage in 1905. Marconi's devotion to his work and their long separations had taken a toll. Marconi also enjoyed the company of other women, and his wife was hurt when she saw signs of his affairs. During the trip, Marconi was, as his daughter Degna recalls, attentive and devoted to his wife. Beatrice enjoyed her visit to Stockholm and collected autographs from the Crown Prince and Princess and from the Nobel laureates she met there, including author Selma Lagerlof, who won the prize for literature.

To Marconi, the prize meant that he had been recognized as a serious scientist, as well as an inventor. At the banquet held on December 10, the evening before the award ceremony, Marconi expressed his pleasure in receiving the prize: "Thanks to the high standing which science has for so long [maintained] and to the impartiality of the Nobel Prize Committee, the Nobel Prize for Physics is rightly considered everywhere as the highest reward within the reach of workers in that branch of Natural Philosophy."[7]

CHAPTER EIGHT

PROGRESS AND PROBLEMS

In the wake of his triumphant trip to Sweden, Marconi faced more threats to his business, which was finally recovering from its financial crisis. First came the threat of a lawsuit. The Anglo-American Telegraph Company claimed that it had an exclusive legal right to operate telegraphy, both wired and wireless, in Newfoundland, which was still under British rule. In response, Marconi moved his station to Glace Bay, Nova Scotia, in Canada. From this new location, he and his assistants conducted more transatlantic tests.

Other legal battles began when companies did not want to obtain Marconi's permission and pay him a fee in order to reproduce his equipment. Furthermore, scientist-inventor Nikola Tesla was bitter that Marconi had won the Nobel Prize. In 1915, he sued Marconi's company for patent infringement, but he lacked enough money to pursue his case. Years later, this case would be reopened. In the meantime, wireless continued to expand with new advances in technology and applications.

Marconi knew that he must continue to improve his inventions if he wanted more people to use wireless. The signals that came through between England and America were less clear than signals from the transatlantic telegraph cable. Overseas radiotelegraphy had a significant problem: interference. The early equipment discharging electricity within the circuit and between the electrodes was unstable. New and improved alternators with higher frequencies reduced interference. The development of a horizontal directional aerial in 1905 and a timed spark system in 1912 enhanced the system still further.

In 1904, the British electrical engineer John A. Fleming invented the two electrode (diode) tube or valve, which could receive radio signals. Then, in 1906, American Lee De Forest brought out his triode, which outperformed the diode. This device, and the ability to tune in to increasingly narrow wavelength bands, made it possible to transmit stronger signals. People could use loudspeakers instead of headphones when they listened to messages.

Major Edwin Howard Armstrong made improvements in the tube that helped the radio to pick up desired signals and screen out unwanted noises. He filed the patent on this new tube, the regenerative receiver circuit, on October 29, 1913. Irving Langmuir of General Electric also came up with this idea, but Armstrong patented his device first. That same year, German inventor Alexander Meissner combined a triode with an oscillator to generate much more powerful signals.

Developments like these paved the way for sending

other kinds of sounds, including speech and music. The year that de Forest introduced his triode, radio operators at sea heard music and a man's voice broadcast over a wireless system. The voice belonged to Reginald A. Ressenden, a native of Quebec, Canada, who set up a telephone transmitter at Brant Rock, Massachusetts, as part of his National Electric Signaling Company. Radio-equipped ships within several hundred miles of Brant Rock said that they heard this program. Ressenden had worked with the General Electric Company to develop a high-frequency continuous wave generator. De Forest's vacuum tube, which was also used for long telephone lines, replaced Ressenden's equipment.

People disagreed, however, about whether Ressenden's was the first transmission of a human voice. Some people claimed that an earlier voice transmission took place in 1892 near Murray, Kentucky, and was spoken by Natan B. Stubblefield, who said "Hello, Rainey."[1]

By 1910, Marconi had adequate technology to propose a large-scale plan he called "The Imperial Wireless Scheme." He suggested that a network of radio stations be set up to connect different countries in the British Empire, including India, England, and Canada. To sell this plan to the British government, Marconi offered to charge them only half of what it cost to send a telegraph. The government concluded that wireless would give them a big advantage during wartime, when an enemy might cut telegraph cables. They suggested that Marconi develop a London-based global communications network that could direct the movements of the Royal Navy.

Two years later, Marconi negotiated a contract to start

developing these wireless stations for the navy. Britain agreed to pay the cost of building these stations and to pay the company fees based on usage. In turn, Marconi agreed that the government would own the stations.

That same year saw the company growing. A larger new headquarters called Marconi House opened in London, and a new Marconi factory opened in Chelmsford, Essex, in England. This allowed the company to increase its staff and produce more equipment. Marconi and his team of scientists found a new way to generate continuous waves called the "multiple sparks system" and he patented his timed spark system for generating continuous waves. That summer, while visiting Italy, he received a warm reception from the king of his homeland.

Late that summer, however, Marconi had a serious accident. He and Beatrice were traveling along a winding road in Italy, with Marconi at the wheel. They hit another vehicle head-on, and both cars were demolished. Marconi was the only one with severe injuries. The hospital issued a report that described his condition: "Serious contusions to the right eyeball and because of the serious swelling, examination is difficult and prognosis is uncertain."[2] The eye was so damaged that doctors had to remove it. Marconi also could not see out of his left eye, but vision returned after a few weeks.

He was also upset about what became known as the "Marconi Company Scandal." Rumors spread that a bribe had been used to obtain the contract for his "Imperial Wireless Scheme." Some government officials were accused of wrongfully buying shares of stock in Marconi's company, based on their knowledge that a lucrative contract would be

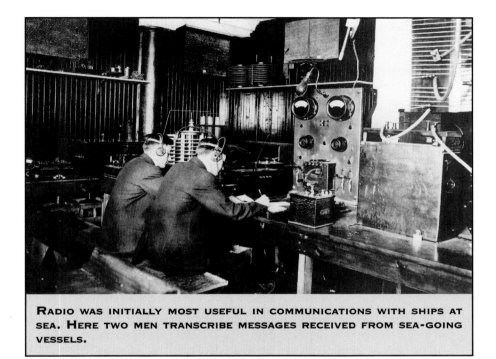

RADIO WAS INITIALLY MOST USEFUL IN COMMUNICATIONS WITH SHIPS AT SEA. HERE TWO MEN TRANSCRIBE MESSAGES RECEIVED FROM SEA-GOING VESSELS.

signed. Marconi's company was cleared, and he himself was not accused of any wrongdoing, but he was embarrassed to be associated with what became known as the "Marconi Scandals." His daughter Degna later wrote, "To the end of his life Father was wracked with anger at this abuse of his name. . . . Whatever his faults, he was invariably just in his dealings with others and for himself he expected no less from the world."[3]

In 1913, by which time Marconi and his family had moved to Rome, a new contract was signed. However, when World War I broke out in 1914, the stations were not yet ready to operate, and the project was dropped. Marconi felt somewhat cheered, as well as vindicated, when Britain's

King George V made him a knight of the Grand Cross Royal Victorian Order.

Wireless assumed new roles during the war, which lasted from 1914–1918. When the war began, Marconi left Britain for Italy. He was considered to be a "foreigner" in Britain, even though Italy was a neutral country. Italy joined the Allies in 1915, and Marconi enlisted in the Italian Army as an officer. He was commissioned as a lieutenant and later promoted to captain. In 1916 he was transferred to the Navy with the rank of Commander Marconi.

Wireless helped the war effort. By 1914, the Marconi-Bellini-Tosi Apparatus for finding ships in foggy weather was operating. Radiotelephonic instruments using triode valves allowed Marconi to provide more efficient radiotelephonic service. The military experimented with ground-to-aircraft radiotelephony—telephone that uses radio for its transmission. During the war years, radiotelephony was used mostly to follow events and direct the movements of troops and supplies. During 1916, Marconi worked on the first VHF radios, which were designed to reduce the problems of using long waves in military operations.

Two breakthroughs occurred in 1915 during the war. A speech was transmitted from New York City to San Francisco, and the first transatlantic voice transmission took place that same year. It went from a naval radio station in Arlington, Virginia, to the Eiffel Tower in Paris, France.

After the war, Marconi continued to serve the government. Because of his international reputation and skills in public relations, he was appointed as a member of the Italian government mission to the United States in 1917.

While governments and the military were using more wireless services, the public was hearing more about its uses, too. In 1910 people heard of a major event via radio for the first time when radio announcers reported the death of King Edward VII.

That same year, wireless helped to arrest a murderer. Dr. Hawley Harvey Crippen, an American-born dentist, had killed his wife in their home in North London, and then fled to Antwerp, Belgium, with his mistress Ethel Le Neve. After police discovered the body, they found traces of poison in her blood. They knew that this same substance was available to medical practitioners, who used it in small doses to treat travel sickness. Suspecting Dr. Crippen, they began searching for him. By then, he and his mistress were heading toward Canada on the steamship *Montrose*, posing as "Mr. Robinson and son." When the captain heard a broadcast news bulletin and noticed their suspicious behavior, he sent a wireless message to British police. An inspector from Scotland Yard went to Canada, where he arrested the couple when the ship arrived. Crippen, who was later found guilty and executed, thus became the first criminal to be caught because of a wireless message.

Another highly publicized use of wireless during this era impressed the public and led to changes in international law. Wireless had shown its value at sea. Beginning in the early 1900s, some ocean-going vessels began to carry wireless equipment. However, this was mainly to carry commercial messages, including personal and business communications to and from the passengers, and the news, which also earned more profits for the company. These messages were called MarconiGrams.

In 1912, wireless saved hundreds of lives. On April 14, the luxury ship *Titanic* sank in the North Atlantic on its first and only voyage. The *Titanic* was the world's largest ship, and had been built in such a way that some people called it "unsinkable." Yet it could not withstand the forces of nature. During the day that it sank, the two Marconi operators in the wireless room had received warnings from other ships stating that an ice field lay ahead. They posted these reports at the message center so that Captain Smith and other crewmembers could see them and take action. They decided to continue on course, however. When the lookout spotted the iceberg at around 11:40 P.M., the crew could not turn the ship fast enough to avert danger. It struck an iceberg and began to sink after the impact.

Aboard the ship, in the wireless room, the two operators tapped out this message: "We've struck a berg. Sinking fast. Come to our assistance. Position, latitude 41.46 north, longitude 50.14 west. MGY."[4] This SOS alerted the *Carpathia*, a passenger ship located 58 miles southeast of the sinking *Titanic*. The *Carpathia* changed direction and rescued 705 survivors before they died on lifeboats and rafts on the icy ocean.

When the *Carpathia* arrived in New York City with the Titanic survivors on board, Guglielmo Marconi was one of only a few people permitted to go aboard. Ironically, Marconi and his wife had been planning to sail on the *Titanic* themselves. Marconi had decided to take another ship in order to reach New York days earlier for a business appointment. As for Beatrice, she changed her plans at the last minute after their son became ill. When Marconi boarded the *Carpathia*, he expressed his sympathy to the survivors, then spent time talking with radio operator Harold Bride, who managed to survive the ordeal. The *Titanic* survivors gave Marconi a gold medal as a way of thanking him for the fact that a wireless was on board the ship. Without it, all of the passengers might have died at sea.

Though the tragedy took 1,503 lives, people were keenly aware that the remaining 705 passengers might also have perished without wireless radio. After the *Titanic* sank, new international regulations required that all ocean-going ships have a working wireless on board. Marconi's company added more Marconi Wireless Schools throughout the world in order to train operators.

From November 12, 1913, to January 20, 1914, the "Safety of Life at Sea" conference was held in London, and sixty-five countries sent representatives.

They adopted sweeping new regulations that required that all large ships, whether powered by motor or sails, must have radios powered at all times. Wireless was now a critical part of safety at sea, not just a way to exchange commercial or friendly messages. For the sea-loving Marconi, there could be no better use for his wireless.

CHAPTER NINE

CHANGES

By 1914, Marconi had witnessed many changes in the science and technology of the wireless, and he had played a major role. Though wireless equipment remained bulky, it could reliably convey messages over long distances and in different kinds of weather, both day and night. For more than ten years, tuning devices had made it possible for a particular operator to use a certain wave band, leaving other bands free for different operators. This meant that wireless radio could expand, especially at sea. But Marconi controlled the key patents, so he maintained a monopoly on the business, which limited the expansion of wireless. Marconi had long insisted that nobody except his company's own operators could use Marconi equipment, and these operators were forbidden to communicate with stations that Marconi had not licensed.

Marconi saw that this policy could not last indefinitely and, by 1912, he began to ease restrictions. The policies were changed anyway, when officials met that year at the international conference held three months after the *Titanic* disaster. New laws required ships and shore stations to communicate no matter whose equipment they were using or where their operators had trained.

After World War I, Marconi focused on new scientific endeavors. He and his staff studied better ways to transmit the human voice by radio. His company linked England and Australia with radio, which meant that radio had now moved around the globe.

Marconi also continued his diplomatic activities on behalf of the Italian government. He received awards for his wartime service, and Italy asked him to serve as a delegate to the Paris Peace Conference. The conference was held in 1919 to officially end World War I and address problems in post-war Europe. He felt frustrated by the conference and feared that Europe remained unstable, with the rise of communism in Russia and a poor economy in war-torn Germany. He also thought Italy did not receive enough credit for its wartime contributions. Marconi confided to his family, "It seems to me very bad after such a war as this that a wave of brutality should be passing over Europe."[1]

His family also noticed that he seemed moody and was sometimes depressed. His daughter Degna later wrote, "To Mother, he confessed that he had lost all desire to go on living—he was convinced that his creative faculties were failing. After these bouts of melancholy, he rebounded violently into brilliantly creative phases."[2]

Marconi's spirits rose when he fulfilled a life-long dream. By 1919, Marconi had become wealthy, and he used some of that wealth to buy a yacht that would serve as both a home on the sea and a floating laboratory. His 220-foot

(60 m) yacht weighed 700 tons and had been built in Scotland for an Austrian aristocrat. It required a crew of at least thirty. Marconi changed the name to *Elettra*, and had the yacht refitted for his purposes. In addition to comfortable quarters and elegant entertaining spaces, he designed spaces for scientific work and experiments. Marconi enjoyed "the good life" and liked to entertain friends, associates, and dignitaries aboard his yacht, but nobody else was allowed inside his radio laboratory.

Marconi kept busy with his work, social life, and various sports, such as golf, and he was known as a good-humored friend. His marriage was going through troubled times, however. Over the years, he had spent long periods of time away from Beatrice and the children. He continued to have affairs with other women, which caused more pain to his wife. She had tried to ignore these relationships, which always came to an end. The war years had brought the family closer, as they faced danger and destruction together and lived as a family at a villa outside Rome. Shortly after the war, a severe influenza epidemic swept through Italy, causing more fear and deaths. The family survived, but some people working at the villa perished.

After the war, Marconi announced that he planned to sell the villa, which Beatrice and the children had come to regard as a safe, stable home. They had learned to love that home, and Beatrice had worked hard to make it beautiful and inviting. Reluctantly, she agreed that they would live with Marconi on the yacht, but she was sad and disappointed to leave her home behind.

Before they set out to sea, Marconi received a telegram with tragic news: His mother had died in London of a heart attack. Twelve days later, he dedicated the first radiophonic transmission from his station in Chelmsford in her honor. It was a concert by Dame Nellie Melba, a world-famous Australian singer.

When Beatrice Marconi joined her husband and other guests on board the *Elettra*, she realized that her husband's mistress was also a fellow passenger. During the voyage, Marconi carried out successful radiotelegraph tests at sea, but his marriage came to an end. When the trip was over, Beatrice and the three children moved into Rome's Hotel de Russie. In 1923, she divorced Marconi and married a member of the Italian nobility. She and Marconi would remain on good terms in the years that followed.

MARCONI (FAR RIGHT) TRANSCRIBES THE FIRST WIRELESS TELEPHONE MESSAGE ON JANUARY 15, 1923.

Marconi was greeted by music coming from wireless when he arrived in New York City to attend a meeting in June 1922. In his speech for members of the American Institute of Electrical and Radio Engineers, he talked about the future of wireless. He announced that new types of marine radio equipment would emit electrical waves and then rebound from metal objects. This information, said Marconi, would "thereby reveal the presence and bearing of ships, even though these ships be unprovided with any kind of radio."[3] The technology Marconi described came to be called radio detection and ranging, or "radar." His company went on to help to develop the techniques for radar at sea.

Further progress was evident later that year when a two-way radio conversation took place between Deal Beach, New Jersey, and the SS *America*, which was 400 miles away at sea. Public radiotelephone service on the high seas would begin seven years later, in 1929. By then, technology enabled stations to contact ships up to 1,500 miles from shore.

Between 1922 and 1924, Marconi conducted a series of experiments to explore the use of short waves rather than long waves. He planned and carried out some major experiments on short waves between Poldhu and his yacht *Elettra*, which was moored for a while on the islands of Palo Verde about 4,000 km from the Poldhu station. These trials led to the development of the so-called "beam system" for long-distance communication. By 1924, Marconi had developed short-wave directional transmission on his yacht and confirmed that it surpassed the long-wave system.

Short-wave wireless communication used less power than long-wave wireless, so it was less expensive to build and operate. Marconi later said, "I saw that the future of radio lay in short waves and reflectors. It took courage to go back, after the expenditure of vast sums of money on long-wave stations . . . [but] . . . near the great cumbersome long-wave stations I built short-wave ones."[4]

Radio broadcasts began in the 1920s, too. The programs included news and music. This would expand during the next thirty years to bring people a variety of programs—news, interviews, speeches, drama, music, and variety shows. The police and the armed forces began using radio, too, as did passenger airlines.

Meanwhile, new theories replaced some of the ideas that had been widely accepted when Marconi began his work back in the 1800s. The theory of the "ether," which James Maxwell had set forth in the late 1860s, was set aside in an article for the July 1922 issue of *Popular Radio*. Charles Proteus Steinmetz wrote, "There are no ether waves; radio and light waves are merely properties of an alternating electromagnetic field of force which extends through space."[5]

In 1924, Marconi revived the idea he had proposed before World War I for an Imperial Wireless Scheme for Great Britain. This plan, however, was based on a short-wave system. In taking on such a challenge, Marconi faced the chance that his company would be financially ruined. The contract stated that if the system did not work properly, the company would pay all the costs involved in building and setting it up.

Would his old dream of a global communications network work? His experiments on short-wave transmission had convinced him that it would. A big step occurred on

May 30, 1924, when the first transmission of a human voice between Poldhu and Sydney, Australia, was heard. Using new technology, Marconi and his staff were able to send messages over 4,130 km using only twelve kilowatts of power. This was much less power than they would need to send messages via long-wave technology.

In October 1926, messages were sent via short-wave equipment between Canada and Britain. The company went on to build and operate stations in India, Australia, South Africa, and the United States. The gamble had paid off. The stations worked, and, after nearly twenty years, the imperial radiotelegraph system was a reality.

Now fifty-two years old, Marconi rejoiced in his new achievement. The effects of wireless were all around him. Radio was now also a part of everyday life for many people. In America, for example, about 2.5 million radio sets were operating in 1924—up from about 500 in 1919. The number of broadcast stations had risen to more than 600. Marconi felt sure that more advances were possible, and he hoped to be a part of them.

CHAPTER TEN

LAST YEARS

By the 1920s, Marconi's reputation as a brilliant inventor and scientist was firmly established. Many people also called him a hero after the wireless saved lives during the famous *Titanic* disaster. He continued to serve as a "goodwill ambassador" for Italy.

In 1926, crowds of cheering people from Marconi's hometown came out to greet him when he returned to Bologna for the 30th anniversary of his first radio patent. The restaurants served "spaghetti a la Marconi" and "wireless pasta" in honor of his momentous achievement.

Marconi remained loyal to his homeland, which now had a fascist government led by General Benito Mussolini. The political climate in Italy had been changing since World War I ended. Marconi hoped that Mussolini would fulfill his pledges to restore law and order, build the Italian economy and national pride, and prevent communism. He joined the Fascist party in 1923, the first time he ever belonged to any political party, and Mussolini thanked him for his support. In 1928, he named Marconi the president of Italy's C.N.R. (National Research Council).

As time went on, Marconi privately began to question Mussolini's policies. His doubts intensified during the 1930s, though he did not publicly oppose Mussolini and felt a strong sense of patriotism. He continued to undertake diplomatic missions at Mussolini's request.

In the meantime, Marconi kept busy with new experiments and business activities. He spent time with his three children from his first marriage and led an active social life.

In 1925, Marconi met and fell in love with a young woman named Maria Cristina Bezzi-Scali, called "Cristina," and he decided to marry again. She was the daughter of an Italian count with connections to the Vatican, the home of the Roman Catholic Pope and seat of Catholicism. Marconi, who had been raised in his mother's Protestant faith, was willing to convert to Catholicism in order to marry Bezzi-Scali, but a larger obstacle stood in their way: Her parents would not let her marry a divorced man, nor could a divorced person be married in the Catholic Church.

Marconi asked his former wife Beatrice to help him obtain an official annulment of their marriage. This meant that church officials would declare their marriage "null," as if it had never happened. As grounds for this annulment, they both declared that at the time of their marriage, they had felt "reservations," and each thought they could get a divorce if the marriage did not work out. The annulment was granted.

Marconi and Bezzi-Scali were married in a Catholic ceremony on June 15, 1927. Once again, prominent people attended the ceremony and reception. Years later, Cristina

Marconi called it "the wedding of the century."[1] The couple divided their time between Marconi's yacht and their country home near Rome. Their daughter, Elettra, was born in 1930.

Shortly after his marriage, Marconi had an angina attack. This heart condition, in which vessels become blocked and thus fail to carry enough blood to the heart, had also afflicted his mother. This first attack of chest pain occurred in November 1927, and other heart attacks would follow. Although doctors urged him to slow down, he refused to stop working.

As had been true his whole life, Marconi had more scientific questions. He continued his experiments with short waves and, during the 1930s, he studied the propagation characteristics of these waves. This paved the way for the development of the world's first microwave radiotelephone link, in Rome. It connected Vatican City with the Pope's summer residence at Castel Gandolfo in 1933. After Marconi personally supervised the installation, he spoke into the microphone, saying, "The first application of microwaves fills my heart both as an Italian and as a scientist with pride and hope for the future."[2]

The previous year, Marconi had launched the Vatican Radio Station. More parts of the world were linked with radiotelephony—for example, in 1931, North and South America were connected.

Long-distance signals also were used in new ways. In March 1930, while on board the *Elettra* in a harbor at Genova, Italy, Marconi sent a signal that lit the town hall in Sydney, Australia, 14,000 miles away. In October he lit the

THE HOME RADIO BUSINESS BOOMED IN THE 1920S. HUNDREDS OF COMMERCIAL RADIO STATIONS BEGAN BROADCASTING SPORTS EVENTS, NEWS, AND MORE. MILLIONS OF FAMILIES BOUGHT RADIOS LIKE THE ONE ABOVE TO ENJOY IN THE COMFORT OF THEIR OWN HOMES.

famous statue of the Redeemer in the harbor at Rio de Janiero, Brazil, via a device called the Coltano repeater.

The year 1935 saw the first telephone call made around the world, using a combination of wire and radio circuits. Until 1936, a transatlantic call to the United States had to be routed through Europe. That changed after a direct radiotelephone circuit was opened in Paris.

Radio was now being used so widely around the world that the air was jammed with signals. To improve that situation, Marconi and other scientists and inventors worked on reflecting radios that could operate on frequencies below one meter. He demonstrated the possibility of using microwaves to communicate a distance of about 36 km between the Italian cities of Santa Margherita Ligure and Levanto, then carried out experiments between his yacht and Rocca di Papa at a distance of 224 km. His later experiments covered still greater distances.

Marconi continued to work on his microwave radio beacon for ship navigation. Like radio waves, microwaves are electromagnetic, but they have shorter wavelengths, ranging from 1 mm to about 30 cm. He began demonstrating the principles of radar, something that he had begun to discuss publicly in the 1920s. In 1935, he gave a dramatic presentation of radar in action. He propelled the *Elettra* into the narrow and hazardous harbor at Sestri Levante, Italy, at full speed. Although the windows on the yacht's bridge were totally blocked, the yacht moved safely through the harbor without hitting anything. Radar had made this possible. This was to be Marconi's last major public demonstration.

During the last decade of his life, Marconi continued to

amass new honors. In 1929, King Victor Emmanuel III gave him the hereditary title of Marchese (Marquis). The Pope awarded him the Grand Cross of the Order of Pius XI. In September 1930, Marconi was named President of the Italian Royal Academy, and two years later, he received the order of the Knight of the Grand Cross of St. Mauritius and St. Lazarus. He also received a coveted scientific prize when the famous physicist Lord Rutherford presented him with the Kelvin gold medal that same year. Another gold medal, from the National Italian Lifeboat Society, called him "the prophet of radio, savior of ships and men."[3]

Slowed down by his heart condition, Marconi reduced his work schedule but did continue to lecture and make public appearances. He spent more time with his four children and was rarely apart from wife Cristina. The couple embarked on a world tour that would last from summer 1933 to early 1934. During their travels, President Roosevelt invited Marconi to the White House. In California, the Marconis attended parties with actors and other celebrities. Marconi was an honored guest at "Marconi Day" at the Chicago World's Fair. In Asia, they met the Emperor of Japan.

The strain of the trip brought on another heart attack in September. It struck at a conference in Vienna, where Marconi discussed the practical uses of microwaves in medicine as a form of physical therapy used to generate heat. As he finished his speech, he felt the familiar pain in his chest. He suffered yet another attack in December during a visit to London and Scotland. Afterwards, his health steadily worsened.

Marconi died of a heart attack in Rome on July 20, 1937.

Radio stations around the world stayed silent for two minutes as a tribute. His casket was placed in a government palace in Rome and thousands of mourners filed past. In newspapers around the world, obituaries praised Marconi as a scientist, inventor, researcher, experimenter, and scholar, as well as a Nobel laureate. The *London Times* commented, "What other men had been content to prove impossible, he accomplished; this is surely greatness."[4]

The controversies over Marconi's patents did not end with his death. Nikola Tesla and his supporters continued to claim that Tesla had discovered wireless technology first and should be considered as the real inventor. During the 1890s, Tesla had developed coils that could transmit and receive powerful radio signals when they were tuned to the same frequency. Early in 1895, he was ready to transmit a signal across a distance of 50 miles in New York State, but that year his lab and work were destroyed when the building caught fire.

A few months after Tesla died in 1943, the United States Supreme Court finally upheld his patent #645,576. This meant that Marconi's patents were invalidated. The court had spent more than a year investigating the case and studying patent records and scientific publications before they issued their opinion. The case became known as the Great Radio Controversy.

Some people applauded this controversial decision, while others said the court's action was selfish and financially motivated. During World War I, Marconi's company had sued the U.S. government for the use of its patents during the war, so restoring Tesla's patent over Marconi's helped their case. This debate continues today.

Wireless and the science that made it possible have affected our lives in many ways. Within years after Marconi's death, radio broadcasts could be found throughout the world. During World War II, radio played a key role for both the Allies and Axis nations. New developments in radar and sonar (locating objects by reflected sound waves) were critical to the war effort. The military could use radar and sonar to identify planes, ships, and other objects, including submarines. Air traffic controllers use radar every day.

Television evolved from wireless technology. In 1923, the first picture was transmitted by wire, in the form of a test photo sent from Washington to Baltimore. The next year, the first transatlantic radiophoto relay took place. The Radio Corporation of New York (later called RCA) beamed a picture of Charles Evans Hughes from London to New York. In 1926, RCA initiated regular radiophoto service. During the 1950s, television became increasingly popular and people could see as well as hear the programs. Within a few years, TV had become part of daily life for people in most parts of the world.

Radio waves also are part of portable radios, car radios, astronomy, radio-microphones, espionage equipment, walkie-talkies, automatic garage-door openers, stereo tuners, and space communications. For example, the VLA Radio Telescope picks up radio waves produced by quasars and other bodies deep in space. Microwaves are used in cooking. They can also carry television programs between land stations a certain distance apart. They can beam signals to and from orbiting satellites.

Besides providing news, information, and entertainment,

this technology is a major part of the economy. According to Ray Minchiello, Chairman of The Guglielmo Marconi Foundation, U.S.A., "the radio, wireless and electronics industry provides the greatest number of jobs in the history of civilization."[5]

More than a century later, how do people view Marconi's contributions as a scientist and inventor? He did not develop a new scientific theory or make something entirely "new." Yet he certainly was determined to discover natural phenomena for himself and pursued a goal that the world's top scientists called "impossible." After his transatlantic triumph in December 1901, Sir Oliver Lodge said, "Marconi's creation, like that of a poet who gathers the words of other men in a perfect lyric, was none the less brilliant and original. . . . It constituted an epoch in human history, on its physical side, and was an astonishing and remarkable feat."[6]

In one of its publications, the U.S. Navy commented, "Marconi can scarcely be called an inventor. His contribution was more in the fields of applied research and engineering development. He possessed a very practical business acumen, and he was not hampered by the same driving urge to do fundamental research which had caused Lodge and Popoff to procrastinate in the development of a commercial [radio] system."[7]

One author summed up his contributions this way: "Guglielmo Marconi did not 'invent' radio—Faraday, Maxwell, Hertz, Lodge, Righi, and Tesla had something to do with it. Marconi can only be regarded as having 'invented' (in 1896) wireless telegraphy, the amplifying valve (1906), and the modulation of a signal over a carrier wave. . . . [he] pioneered wireless technology, becoming the father of radio and the grandfather of cellphones."[8]

Marconi has been praised for his business skills, which enabled him to spread the use of wireless. Biographer Giancarlo Masini writes, "Marconi was also a remarkable captain of industry, a formidable organizer of research and production. He was a gifted 'talent-scout,' capable of gathering around himself the best minds and the most gifted young men."[9] His company, which is today called GEC-Marconi, is a giant multinational corporation that works in

TODAY, SATELLITE RADIO ALLOWS A PERSON TO LISTEN TO THE SAME STATION BROADCASTS FROM COAST TO COAST OF THE UNITED STATES.

the areas of aerospace, defense, broadcasting, radar, and satellite communications.

Masini also notes that Marconi can be regarded as a great man of science "if by science we also mean applied research for practical purposes,"[10] since he was "able to conceive and manufacture with his own hands, often with rudimentary tools and instruments, and with no scientific theory outlined in advance."[11]

The Nobel Committee recognized these attributes and achievements when they awarded the prize to Marconi in 1909. Without Marconi's intelligence, foresight, persistence, and business skills, the development and progress of wireless might have been quite different and much slower. Few inventions have had such a profound effect on human history.

ACTIVITIES

A World of Sounds

Throughout his life, Guglielmo Marconi asked questions and looked for answers, even when other scientists thought he was on the wrong track. To discover 'how things work,' he became a keen observer and conducted experiments with materials that he found in his home or outdoors, as well as in the lab. As he reached his teens, Marconi was chiefly interested in learning more about sound and how sounds are transmitted.

The Vibrations Around Us

We hear sound when an object vibrates—moves back and forth quickly—in matter. This matter can be a solid, a liquid, or a gas—anything that can be made to vibrate. When a vibration moves through matter, it causes tiny molecules in the matter around it to move. In turn, these particles move other particles, a process that moves the vibration along in what we call a sound wave. We hear a bell, for example, when someone moves it to cause the ringing. The sound waves from the bell move through the atmosphere.

Think about the sounds you hear in a typical day. During a period of ten minutes, while standing outdoors or in the hallway at school, how many different sounds can you identify? Do these sounds come from nearby or far away? What characteristics make one sound different from another? Why can we hear some sounds but not others?

With a spoon and a piece of string, you can hear sound vibrations that are too weak to be picked up by the human ear alone. Tie some string to the handle of a spoon, then hold the other end of the string firmly against the center of your ear while the spoon hangs down. Tap the spoon. Do you hear a bell-like sound? What happens when you repeat this activity with other objects tied to a string? Can you hear the sound if you don't place the string against your ear?

In an open space, sound waves spread out from the source in various directions. We can hear sounds across longer distances if the waves are not allowed to spread out so much in the open air. Try speaking quietly while your friend stands at the end of the yard or driveway. Can he or she hear you? Now speak in the same way through one end of a garden hose while your friend holds the other end of the hose to his or her ear. What happened this time?

Changes in Pitch

Sounds differ in terms of their amplitude (degree of loudness) and pitch (high versus low). Try changing the pitch of the noises made by a vibrating ruler. First, place a flexible ruler on the edge of a table or desk so that more than half of the ruler sticks out from the edge. Now hold one end firmly on the table and snap the other end of the ruler and listen. Repeat this experiment, so that less of the ruler is extending over the edge each time. How does the pitch of the noise change, depending on how much ruler is off the table when you 'hit' it?

When the longer parts of the ruler are vibrating, the pitch is lower. The frequency of the vibrations changed, depending on the length of the vibrating part. Longer vibrating parts have a smaller frequency. The smaller the frequency, the lower the pitch. With greater frequency, the pitch is higher.

Maybe you have tried filling your lungs with helium from an inflated balloon and then spoken some words? Your voice sounds higher pitched than normal. Why? Sound travels faster in helium than it does in regular air. Since helium has less mass than the normal atmosphere, the collisions among molecules that transmit sound energy occur more rapidly.

Other things can affect pitch, too. In a guitar, for example, the mass of a string, its tightness, and the length affect the frequency of the vibration, and, therefore, the pitch. Think about what creates the sounds you hear when various musical instruments are played. Something in the instrument must vibrate—either a solid part, the air, or both. With some instruments, musicians vibrate their lips to produce distinctive sounds. As you examine various instruments, think about which part is vibrating. For example, on a violin, the strings are made to vibrate. Flute players use their lips to create different sounds and and control the intensities of those sounds while changing the amount of air that flows through the body of the flute.

From Ear to Brain

The human ear has three main parts that enable us to hear sounds. The outer ear—made up of the visible part of the ear—picks up sound waves. They pass through the ear canal to the eardrum, which vibrates in the presence of sound waves. These waves are then passed along to three tiny bones in the middle ear which carry vibrations to the inner ear (cochlea). Thousands of tiny sound receptors in the cochlea transmit signals to the hearing nerve. This nerve carries them to the brain, which interprets various sounds.

You can use a table fork to hear sound vibrations. Tap

the fork (tine side down) on the table, then quickly hold it against your outer ear. Do you hear the sounds? Now try tapping the fork again. But this time, place the handle on the bone just behind your ear. The vibrations travel from that bone to your inner ear. Now try tapping the fork again, and this time bite down on the handle. The sound vibrations move through your teeth and bones to your ear. These sounds should sound even louder than those you heard when you put the fork to your ear.

Early Distance Communication

Before people could transmit voices over wires, or even without wires, they found ways to send signals across distances. Some signals were made with sounds, such as drumbeats. People also signaled to each other with light—such as a fire, or, in later years, oil lamps (lighthouse signals), and then electrical lights. The Morse code system of dots and dashes can be sent out visually, using light, as well as through a telegraph system. Try signaling to a friend at night using flashlights. Together, make a "code" in which long or short bursts of light mean different words or letters. (In Morse code, for example, a long burst of light is a "dash;" a short burst is a "dot.") Or use reflected light from mirrors to signal each other during the day. Use your hand to cover and uncover the mirror as it reflects rays from the sun.

Energy Conductors

Like the scientists who inspired him, Marconi used metal wire in the mechanisms he built to transmit signals. When Michael Faraday built the first generator in 1831, he placed a magnet inside a coil made from copper wire. The current flowed through the wire because copper is a good conductor.

Likewise, Alessandro Volta used copper discs when he made his battery (also called an electric cell) in 1799.

Try this trick with copper pennies. Tell a friend that you want to test your "mind-reading" ability. Before you start, put five pennies in the refrigerator. Each penny should have a different date (year). Give the plate full of pennies to your friend and ask him or her to pick one penny while you close your eyes. The friend should then pick up this penny and hold it very tightly for a minute while memorizing the date. After he or she puts the penny back on the plate, quickly open your eyes and select the correct penny from the plate. You can identify the correct penny by touching them to find the warmest one.

Does metal conduct heat better than wood or plastic? The next time your family is cooking a pot of soup, try stirring it with a metal spoon. Then use a wooden spoon, followed by a plastic spoon. Let each spoon rest in the pot for a minute while you hold it. Does your hand feel hotter when you hold the metal spoon, the wooden spoon, or plastic spoon? Like sound waves, heat is a form of energy.

Will sound waves pass through metal better than through wood? Test this out with a piece of wood, such as a stick, and a piece of metal, such as a rod. These sticks should be about the same length and thickness. Hold one end against your ear and tap the other end with an object, such as a pen. Which material conducts sound better?

Observing . . . asking questions . . . looking for answers . . . these are the qualities that make for an active mind. These qualities keep us alert and open to learn new things— and who knows where that might lead?

CHRONOLOGY

1874—Guglielmo Marconi born April 25, in Bologna, Italy.

1895—Marconi sends the first wireless transmissions at Villa Griffone, near Bologna.

1896—Marconi goes to London to market his wireless and files patent #12039 in June.

1897—The Wireless Telegraph and Signal Company is registered in Britain on July 20.

1899—The first radio factory in the world begins when Marconi's company acquires the Hall Street Works.
Marconi sends messages across a distance of sixty miles; his wireless equipment is used for ship-to-shore communications.

1902—Receives Grand Cross of the Order of the Crown of Italy.

1903—Receives Freedom of the City of Rome award.

1905—Marries Beatrice O'Brien.
Receives the Chevalier of the Civil Order of Savoy.

1907—Initiates a commercial transatlantic wireless service.

1909—Awarded the Nobel Prize for Physics.

1910—First proposes "Imperial Wireless Scheme."

1912—Marconi company "scandal."
Loses eye in automobile accident.

1914—Appointed a Senatore in the Italian Senate and Honorary Knight Grand Cross of the Royal Victorian Order in England.
Appointed as an advisor to Italian Armed Forces.

1917—Goodwill mission to the United States.

1919—Delegate to the Paris Peace Conference.
Buys his yacht *Elettra*.

1923—Joins Fascist party in Italy.
Divorces Beatrice.

1924—Develops the short-wave radio.

1927—Marries Cristina Bezzi-Scali.

1929—Receives the hereditary title of Marchese.

1933–34—World tour.

1935—Carries out last diplomatic mission for Italian government.

1937—Dies July 20, in Rome, of a heart attack.

CHAPTER NOTES

Chapter 1. A Communications Giant

1. H. Hildebrand, Untitled presentation speech for the awarding of the 1909 Nobel Prize in Physics in *Nobel Lectures—Physics 1901–1921, The Nobel Foundation* (Amsterdam, The Netherlands: Elsevier Publishing Company, 1967), p. 193.

2. Trevor I. Williams, *Science: A History of Discovery in the Twentieth Century* (New York: Oxford University Press), p. 30.

3. Marconi Nobel Prize lecture at <http://www.nobel.se/physics/laureates/1909/press.html> (February 24, 2003).

4. H. Hildebrand, presentation speech.

5. Degna Marconi, *My Father Marconi* (New York: McGraw Hill, 1962), p. 190.

6. Ibid.

7. H. Hildebrand, presentation speech.

8. Ibid.

Chapter 2. Big Ears and Big Ideas

1. Degna Marconi, *My Father Marconi* (New York: McGraw Hill, 1962), p. 8.

2. Guglielmo Marconi, Marconi Nobel Prize lecture at <http://www.nobel.se/physics/laureates/1909/press.html> (February 24, 2003).

3. "Michael Faraday (1791–1867): Lectures on the Forces of Matter, 1859," *Modern History Sourcebook*, n.d., <http://www.fordham.edu/halsall/mod/1859Faraday-forces.html> (June 1, 2004).

4. Degna Marconi, p. 14.

5. Carl Van Doren, *Benjamin Franklin* (New York, The Viking Press, 1980), p. 160.

6. Degna Marconi, p. 13.

Chapter 3. A Dream Takes Shape

1. Degna Marconi, *My Father Marconi* (New York: McGraw Hill, 1962), p. 18.

2. Giancarlo Masini, *Marconi* (New York: Marsilio, 1976), p. 33.

3. Ibid.

4. "The Victorian Internet," *Imperial Pulp and Data Corporation*, n.d., <http://eimperial.com/HighTech.htm> (June 1, 2004).

5. "First Electronic Church of America: Heinrich Hertz," n.d., <http://www.webstationone.com/fecha/hertz.htm> (February 24, 2003).

6. "Heinrich Hertz" *Consumer Electronics Association (CEA): Hall of Fame*, n.d., <http://cea.tmghosting.com/publications/hall_of_fame/hertz_h_00.asp> (June 1, 2004).

7. Orrin E. Dunlap, Jr. *Communications in Space* (New York: Harper & Row, 1970), p. 4.

8. H. Hildebrand, Untitled presentation speech for the awarding of the 1909 Nobel Prize in Physics in *Nobel Lectures—Physics 1901–1921, The Nobel Foundation* (Amsterdam, The Netherlands: Elsevier Publishing Company, 1967), p. 1.

9. "Mahlon Loomis's Journal," *American Treasures of the Library of Congress*, December 13, 2002, <http://www.loc.gov/exhibits/treasures/trr083.html> (February 24, 2003).

10. George P. Oslin, *The Story of Telecommunications* (Macon, Ga.: Mercer University Press, 1992), p. 274.

Chapter 4. "On a Good Road"

1. Testimony in the injunction suit of the *Marconi Wireless Telegraph Company of America vs. the National Electric Signaling Company in the U.S. District Court*, Brooklyn, NY, 1913.

2. Orrin E. Dunlap, Jr. *Communications in Space* (New York: Harper & Row, 1970), p. 7.

3. Giancarlo Masini, *Marconi* (New York: Marsilio, 1976), p. 48.

4. Ibid.

5. Degna Marconi, *My Father Marconi* (New York: McGraw Hill, 1962), p. 26.

6. Guglielmo Marconi, Marconi Nobel Prize lecture at <http://www.nobel.se/physics/laureates/1909/press.html> (February 24, 2003).

7. Ibid.

8. Ibid.

9. Degna Marconi, p. 29.

10. Ibid., p. 30.

Chapter 5. Patents and Promotions

1. "Guglielmo Marconi (1874-1937)," n.d., <http://members.rogers.com/4dtv/history/marconi.html> (July 19, 2004).

2. *Guglielmo Marconi*, n.d., <http://webstationone.com/fecha/marconi.htm> (February 24, 2003).

3. Giancarlo Masini, *Marconi* (New York: Marsilio, 1976), p. 64.

4. Ibid., p. 66.

5. Orrin E. Dunlap, Jr., *Communications in Space* (New York: Harper & Row, 1970), p. 8.

6. Masini, p. 99.

7. Ibid., p. 100.

8. Dunlap, p. 10.

Chapter 6. Across the Ocean

1. "First Atlantic Transmissions" n.d., <http://www.marconicalling.com/museum/html/events-I=30=0.html> (February 24, 2003).

2. Degna Marconi, p. 89.

3. H. Hildebrand, Untitled presentation speech for the awarding of the 1909 Nobel Prize in Physics in *Nobel Lectures— Physics 1901–1921, The Nobel Foundation* (Amsterdam, The Netherlands: Elsevier Publishing Company, 1967), p. 208.

4. Giancarlo Masini, p. 150.

5. Degna Marconi, p. 104.

6. Ibid., p. 106.

7. Masini, pp. 157–158.

8. George P. Oslin, *The Story of Telecommunications* (Macon, Ga.: Mercer University Press, 1992), p. 274.

9. Ibid.

10. "The Birth of Wireless," *Print e-Business Report*, August 2002, <http://www.piamidam.org/downloads/0802ebizrpt.pdf> (February 24, 2003).

11. Gioia Marconi Braga, "A Biography of Guglielmo Marconi," *Guglielmo Marconi International Fellowship Foundation of Columbia University*, n.d., <http://www.marconifoundation.org/pages/marconi_editable/marconi_family/bio_by_gioia.htm> (June 1, 2004).

12. Masini, p. 165.

13. Orrin E. Dunlap, Jr., *Communications in Space* (New York: Harper & Row, 1970), p. 12.

Chapter 7. Fame and Family

1. Degna Marconi, *My Father Marconi* (New York: McGraw Hill, 1962), p. 122.

2. Giancarlo Masini, *Marconi* (New York: Marsilio, 1976), p. 167.

3. *PBS Homepage*, n.d., <http://www.pbs.org/tesla/ll/ll_whoradio.html> (February 24, 2003).

4. Degna Marconi, p. 165.

5. "Newspaper Articles Covering the Wedding of Marconi and Beatrice" n.d., <http://www.marconicalling.com/museum/html/objects/newspapers/objects-i=1006.539-t=4-n=0.html> (February 24, 2003).

6. George P. Oslin, *The Story of Telecommunications* (Macon, Ga.: Mercer University Press, 1992), p. 275.

7. "Guglielmo Marconi: Banquet Speech." n.d., <http://www.nobel.se/physics/laureates/1909/marconi-speech.html> (February 24, 2003).

Chapter 8. Progress and Problems

1. "About Radio: Radio History," n.d., <http://inventors.about.com/library/inventors/blradio.htm> (February 24, 2003).

2. Giancarlo Masini, *Marconi* (New York: Marsilio, 1976), p. 268.

3. Degna Marconi, *My Father Marconi* (New York: McGraw Hill, 1962), p. 210.

4. Orrin E. Dunlap, Jr., *Communications in Space* (New York: Harper & Row, 1970), p. 13.

Chapter 9. Changes

1. Degna Marconi, p. 229.

2. Ibid., pp. 229–230.

3. Giancarlo Masini, *Marconi* (New York: Marsilio, 1976), p. 292.

4. Degna Marconi, p. 258.

5. Orrin E. Dunlap, Jr., p. 2.

Chapter 10. Last Years

1. Giancarlo Masini, *Marconi* (New York: Marsilio, 1976), p. 305.

2. Degna Marconi, *My Father Marconi* (New York: McGraw Hill, 1962), p. 289.

3. Masini, pp. 319–320.

4. *DCARCommunicator*, November 1998, <http://www.dcarc.net/news/Vol98n11.pdf> (July 19, 2004).

5. Ray Minchiello, "TITANIC tragedy spawns wireless advancements," n.d., <http://www.marconiusa.org/history/titanic.htm> (February 24, 2003).

6. Orrin E. Dunlap, Jr., *Communications in Space* (New York: Harper & Row, 1970), p. 11.

7. U.S. government publication *History of Communications—Electronics in the United States Navy* (Bureau of Ships and Office of Naval History), 1963.

8. "The Birth of Wireless," *Print e-Business Report*, August 2002, <http://www.piamidam.org/downloads/0802ebizrpt.pdf> (February 24, 2003).

9. Masini, p. 365.

10. Ibid., p. 364.

11. Ibid., p. 365.

FURTHER READING

Birch, Beverley. *Guglielmo Marconi: Radio Pioneer*. San Diego: Blackbirch Press, 2001.

Fleisher, Paul. *Waves: Principles of Light, Electricity, and Magnetism*. Minneapolis: Lerner Books, 2001.

Goldsmith, Mike. *Guglielmo Marconi*. Raintree Steck-Vaughn Publishers, 2003.

Parker, Steve. *Guglielmo Marconi and Radio*. Broomall, Pa.: Chelsea House, 1995.

Skurzynsky, Gloria. *Waves: The Electromagnetic Universe*. Washington, D.C.: National Geographic, 1996.

INTERNET ADDRESSES

Development of Radar
http://www.marconicalling.com/museum/html/events/events-i=64-s=2.html

Through the Wires: Radio Invention
http://library.thinkquest.org/27887/gather/history/radio.shtml

Marconi Foundation
http://www.marconiusa.org

Nobel e-Museum
http://www.nobel.se

INDEX